A4
New Zealand Architects Monograph Series

Architectus

Bowes Clifford Thomson

Series Editor:
Amanda Hyde de Kretser PhD, UNITEC

Edited for Publication by:
John Balasoglou, Balasoglou Books

Contents

A note on the plans

Floor levels follow the convention of the ground floor (or lowest ground floor) being level 1 and upper floors level 2, 3, etc. Obvious basements are labelled as such. The exception being Jade Stadium, where descriptions of the levels seems more sensible.

Plans are reproduced at the following scales:

Te Papa Tongarewa and Jade Stadium are 1:2000

Sciences Library and Population Health Complex are 1:1000

Mathematics Statistics & Computer Science Building and New Lynn Community Centre are 1:750

Netball Court-cover, Teacher Support Services Centre, St Peter's Technology Building, St Peter's Middle School are 1:500

Stanley Point House and 111 Wellesley Street are 1:400

Clifford Forsyth House is 1:200

Creating Opportunities for Architecture

BY TONY VAN RAAT
Head of UNITEC School of Architecture

The practice Architectus: Bowes Clifford Thomson has become known for a series of precise, carefully crafted buildings in New Zealand. It was formed in 1986 by Malcolm Bowes, Patrick Clifford and Michael Thomson who had met at the Auckland University School of Architecture where they studied in the early 1980s. Following graduation they travelled and worked for short periods both overseas and in New Zealand before returning to Auckland. The practice has since then produced a substantial body of work, much of which has been published in the local architectural press and overseas.

During the production of this book Architectus joined with an alliance of Australian practices to form Architectus Pty, and the practice consequently changed their name to Architectus Auckland. There are now Architectus offices in Sydney, Melbourne and Brisbane.

Now, at a time when the practice is transforming itself into a regional entity, is an appropriate time to publish this documentary record of the first stages of the practice's work.

Analysis of any serious body of architecture cannot and should not avoid the question of ideology and how belief systems have been incorporated into building. All architecture is in some sense propositional and the origins of the propositions architects make deserve attention, just as does the built (or buildable) form that they take. The partners of Architectus assert that the ideological foundation of the practice is visible in what they do; this statement in itself reflects a belief in the importance of the systematic development of ideas in architecture and in their manifestation in constructed work.

The work of Architectus is characterised by an underlying concern with developing a critical and rigorous approach to the problem of making architecture. The partners have also been prominent in an empiricist reinterpretation of modernism in New Zealand architecture. This interest in modernism is reflected by close study of precedent, by the use of formal devices – their buildings are commonly subtractive rather than additive in composition – and in the nature of their relationship to technology. In the course of their use and development of modernist themes they have not hesitated to make overt references to iconic modernist projects. Examples of this are most clear in projects such as the Remuera Road apartment, Auckland, with it's Corbusian 'light cannon', and the Canterbury Mathematics Statistics and Computer Sciences Building, in which the treatment of the most prominent façades acknowledges Louis Kahn's work. This is an informed and conscious borrowing, based on study of architectural history and on reflection of themes taken from it.

Architectus also takes a particular position towards the use of materials. It is well known that for interior use, for example, the practice tends where possible to use self-finished materials such as concrete, concrete block and plywood, in preference to plaster board. This carries with it an echo of the words of Peter Zumthor who writes (in *A+U: Peter Zumthor*, February 1998)

"Analysis of any serious body of architecture cannot and should not avoid the question of ideology and how belief systems have been incorporated into building."

"…we must constantly ask ourselves what the use of a particular material could mean in a specific architectural context. Good answers to these questions can throw new light onto both the way the material is generally used and its own inherent sensuous qualities."

The question of ideology is of greater than usual importance in the case of Architectus because of the conscious attitude which the partners have adopted towards it. For a long time in New Zealand, and certainly since well before this practice was founded, few local architects discussed their production with complete candour or insight. What explanation was given tended to be descriptive and to promote the belief – certainly a false one – that architecture emerges naturally either from the conditions of the site or from the brief or the available technology. Seldom was the intellectual content of the work, the systematic development of ideas that informed and motivated it, opened up for discussion.

Architectus has acted consciously to change that. The partners, and particularly Patrick Clifford, have always been prepared to talk about their architecture, to discuss thoughts or concepts that are not just programmatic but which lead into broader themes within the work of the practice: those things that have made a difference. Particularly since the mid-1990s and the success of their Canterbury University projects they have been willing to engage in debate about architecture in general and their own work in particular, and in any forum. In doing this they acknowledge the example of other architects – they particularly name Ian Athfield – who are similarly committed to an active engagement in the discourse on architecture.

By and through its practise Architectus engages in research. There is some current debate about how research can be defined, and indeed whether anything done in a relatively conventional practice can ever be called research. It is therefore necessary to state that research here means more than what might be narrowly, and sometimes esoterically, defined as such by academics. Research can also be manifest in other, broader ways: it can be revealed by reflection, by propositioning, by developing and by testing architecture within a critical and self-conscious environment; research, in fact, embedded in and executed through practice. To propose that practice can be research is not, of course, to suggest that all practise is research. To be considered as research, practise must necessarily be reflective and critical; and it must be placed in the forum of public debate. Simply to build is not to be engaged in research, although the processes necessary to arrive at a point where building is possible may well have included reflection and propositioning and developing and testing. It is in the whole spectrum of activities, and in the framework of reading, involvement with education and public debate which holds it, that the work of a practice can be considered as research. And it is an act of some generosity to reveal the fruits of this research in public discussion. Clifford defines the activity of the practice as follows: "What's the definition of research? If research is going to sources, if it is analysis, if it is review, if it is original thought, then I think that what we do absolutely is research and it results in the production of buildings. We are engaged in analysing existing models. We are familiar with the field. We work vigorously on that and from time to time we think we have the odd original thought!" This is an acceptable definition of practice-based research activity.

The practice has also developed expertise, which is considerable by New Zealand standards, in the field of technical research. This has perhaps been encouraged by the fact that none of the partners worked for other established

"A certain curiosity to do things simply because they're different from what has been done before may also sometimes act as motivation."

practices for any length of time before starting their own office. They have always been inclined, therefore, to confront any new design problem by developing an understanding of it from a foundational level. This can lead to an approach to design that is not merely different from the standard or conventional but which leads to innovations in detailing and construction, which then themselves become significant design generators. A certain curiosity to do things simply because they're different from what has been done before may also sometimes act as motivation. Technical research is important to the practice and the partners are willing to take some risks when developing new systems employed for their buildings: they correctly acknowledge that the clients have shared those risks too.

It is a conscious commitment to the actual in architecture, an actual they are prepared to theorise, that leads in the work of this practice to sophistication without the cleverness that sometimes affects architects who configure their work in accordance with theory. In engagement with the experiential and technical reality of the built work rather than with the hypothetical or the virtual, Architectus involves itself in research and investigation of architecture as a craft, or even as a physical endeavour. There are not necessarily any difficult intellectual concepts involved in such a task (although having a few clues is useful), which is perhaps why some bright graduates find the practice of architecture frustrating. At least a partial remedy for this normal consequence of engaging with the building industry is to try to give each job the best possible chance of success. This is a more reliable proposition than trusting to luck. Architectus, like other top practices, represents the belief that complete commitment to the project gives clients confidence and enhances the prospect of the project being achieved.

The practice has also made some commitment to the social aspect of architecture. It was Zaha Hadid who said that there can be no great architecture without a social programme (in *The End of Architecture*, P Noever (ed), Prestel, Munich, 1992) and the view of Architectus, clearly stated, is that any architect who hasn't got a conception that architecture has a social purpose is in serious trouble. The practice expresses this by the work it has done on social housing and by a desire to undertake more. In projects like the New Lynn Community Centre, or projects in tertiary education, there is also evidence of a broader social agenda for architecture than is contained in the single family house, which has long been, and still largely is, the rather indulgent mainstay of much architectural production in New Zealand.

The practice is perhaps less well known to the general public for sustainable design, but is nevertheless highly conscious of the possibilities that sustainability and good environmental design offer for architecture, especially in larger projects. Quite apart from being a good and indeed necessary thing in itself, the partners of Architectus argue that a commitment to sustainability has the significant strategic benefit of returning authority to the architect. For to be effective sustainable design needs to be embedded throughout the whole of a project, a task which only the architect can fulfil. It is perhaps this ability to see, and sometimes actively to construct opportunities for architecture, that gives the practice its depth and complexity.

Tony van Raat is the Head of the School of Architecture and Landscape Architecture at UNITEC Institute of Technology in Auckland.

"Architectus represents the belief that complete commitment to the project gives clients confidence and enhances the prospect of the project being achieved."

The Pleasure in a Building: Recent Auckland Architecture

DOUGLAS LLOYD JENKINS

"…in Auckland, even monumental architecture must defer to the landscape and therefore usually fails to be at all monumental."

In the 1960s the University of Auckland underwent a period of unprecedented growth. In a comparatively short time, new Engineering, Mathematics, Physics and Chemistry, and Botany buildings were completed, along with a new Student Union building. These projects employed a range of architects, from the Ministry of Works through KRTA to Warren and Mahoney. What bound this seemingly diverse group of buildings (and architects) together was their pursuit of the new monumentalism prevalent internationally (at least on university campuses) during the 1960s.

This monumentalism sits uncomfortably with the direction Auckland architecture subsequently took. In a city in which the better buildings often choose to dissolve, the University buildings of the 1960s have generally been relegated to the category of architectural curiosity. Today they might be entirely 'invisible' were three of these buildings not neighbouring the Auckland University School of Architecture. Only the most hapless architecture student could fail to notice them, thus ensuring they provide some sort of imprint on the architectural imagination of New Zealand architecture.

In part, the tendency for Auckland's larger buildings to attempt some sort of dissolving act comes from a deference to landscape form. The language of Auckland is, we are told, geographical, and buildings don't get much of a look in as symbols of the city. Auckland is a city of cones, a series of volcanoes, and a harbour, connected by an undulating isthmus landscape. This way of thinking about Auckland can be traced partly to the work of Richard Toy and to humanist traditions taught at the Auckland University School of Architecture through the 1960s and 1970s, to which none of the generation that studied there were ever entirely immune.

The result is that in Auckland, even monumental architecture must defer to the landscape and therefore usually fails to be at all monumental. Like the motorway, Auckland buildings snake around the volcanic cones on their way to the suburbs. Here even large public buildings act like houses, possessing a kind of physical flexibility akin to that of the ever expandable family home.

The buildings of Auckland University, along with works of earlier architects like Gummer and Ford (Auckland Railway Station) and Grierson Aimer and Draffin (Auckland Museum), suggest the existence of another loose tradition in Auckland architecture. It is an urban monumentalism encapsulated in the idea that a building is an inescapably tangible and complete object. It is architecture not as an act of commerce, nor as an act of theory, but as the result of an advanced understanding of the craft of building. It is within this tradition that Architectus' recent Auckland work can be contextualised, not only in an attempt to understand its origins but to understand the potential significance of the work now being undertaken.

The significance of the Technology Building at St Peter's College (1999-2001) was not in the addition of another new building in boomtown. It was in the way it indicated a potential shift in the role of architecture within Auckland. Coming as it did in the slipstream of the millennial moment, St Peter's suggested new possibilities for a revived urban architecture in New Zealand's great, dissipated, suburban city.

What initially attracted attention was the way the new St Peter's building refused to ignore the motorway. Previous architecture built along Auckland's southern motorway tended to do exactly that, as if offended by the very presence of such an urban expanse. At St Peter's, with one side of the Technology Building pushed hard up against the road, architecture took on the motorway, on terms determined by the new arrival. The finished building is emphatic; it shifts in concert with the motorway, rather than curving smoothly, and submissively, against the motorway's flank. At the same time it is indisputably an independent object placed alongside the motorway, but together they suggest the beginning of a new dialogue between building and a broader urban landscape.

The motorway could easily have been used as an excuse to create a mute building. Instead the Technology Building signals its intended purpose to passing traffic through shadowy silhouettes of equipment that play against the frosted windows. The building is a sign that has, as intended, come to define the entire school. In this St Peter's conjures up those earlier buildings, like Auckland Museum or the University of Auckland's Mathematics, Physics and Chemistry that need no attached typography, but are in themselves the signs of urban Auckland, referred to by residents of the city in part through their shape. St Peter's is now known to Aucklanders as the building with the inverted white cross that lights up at night. The building then, works for those who will never set foot on the school grounds but who seek an architecturally engaging city.

In signalling the intention of its architects to work on a greater canvas than that provided solely by the client, the Technology Building seemed to suggest a certain optimism about the role of the architect in the future of Auckland architecture. It is interesting then to look at it alongside the New Lynn Community Centre (1999-2001). Also built adjacent to a problematic transport corridor, this time rail, this building again takes on a wider role in the urban environment than simply meeting the client's needs for a replacement community centre.

The New Lynn Community Centre provides a strong architectural focus in a suburb that, although not without quality modern architecture, lacks any focal point other than a ubiquitous shopping mall. By pushing back against the rail corridor and opening the opposite side of the building up through the use of a glass wall and colonnade, the building is given a sense of civic presence. The finished structure is more reminiscent of the traditional idea of a town hall than of a community centre. In this sense it appears as if the question has been asked – what is being requested (a community centre) and what is needed (a central focus for the community)? The building that results places equal importance on answering both questions.

The decision by Architectus to work largely in the field of institutional and civic buildings indicates a willingness to take on the wider social roles of architecture that have by and large fallen away from contemporary practice. That both architectural and social issues are again being dealt with in these buildings seems to point to the dual origins of the firm in a climate in which notions of architectural humanism swirled around built evidence of an urban monumen-

"…it is indisputably an independent object placed alongside the motorway but together they suggest the beginning of a new dialogue between building and a broader urban landscape."

talism. Yet the strong sense of direction from buildings like the New Lynn Community Centre or the buildings on St Peter's, Auckland Grammar or Auckland College of Education campuses, do not act solely as flagships for wider architectural programmes. If these buildings have a macro-purpose they also have a micro agenda.

Architectus' buildings are highly crafted objects, but in the 21st century craft is a problematic word. This is particularly so in Auckland, which was founded on, and has continued to pursue, the notion of speculation as an admirable pursuit. Auckland is a city where architecture comes under twin, and unique, pressures. First there is the pressure of economic expediency driven by speculative commerce (an explanation as to why so many Auckland architects chose to 'specialise' in the house). Second there is a pressure, driven by the architectural schools, to theorise (and to over-theorise) built architecture as a means of gaining academic legitimacy for themselves. Both of these sectors find the notion of craft difficult. To businesses craft infers additional time spent on a project and therefore higher than necessary costs. To the academic, to ally oneself to craft is to take a dangerously under-theorised position, lacking in connection to the published text and seemingly sitting outside the central thrust of architectural thinking, at least as it occurs within the schools.

The result of these pressures is architects (and architecture) who have difficulty in wholly embracing the exploration of craft as a central value in built work. In Architectus' case Patrick Clifford has written, "architecture as craft is not enough – but we believe that the practice of architecture is craft, and we hold that dear." Examine a building like St Peter's Middle School (2001-03) and it becomes clear that one of the very central concerns of the architects is clearly the exploration of the way that materials work together. That is not to say that the materials solely determine actions or forms within a building. However, the pleasure of the building for both architect and end user is in the enjoyment of those individual components. The play of cedar against aggregate panels, the carefully tapered vertical fins in cast concrete (with P10, their component number, still clearly marked in blue chalk on the under-side), and a generously sectioned selection of aluminium joinery, all suggest craftsman-like approaches to creating a building. They suggest time encapsulated in the building itself and therefore suggest permanence. Without this attention it would be difficult to imagine a building like this achieving the spiritual dimension it does.

The result of bringing together components creates what seems a more solid building than has become the norm in Auckland. Take for example the solidity of the Technology Building. This seems somewhat at odds with the general direction of early 21st century Auckland architecture. Even when one explores the entire building, rather than its motorway elevations, and discovers the degree to which the building opens up to its eastern side into a series of colonnaded walkways and glass-lined classrooms and workshops, the building seems to take its architectural markers from the more solid and crafted architecture of the South Island. Other recent Auckland architecture has not been marked with the same sense of permanence. Humanism led to something more transient dominating architectural form.

How then does one fit buildings that seem to explore the central notions of craft, permanence and social purpose within the spread of 21st century Auckland architecture? At one level the exploration of such values seems 'old fashioned'. That is to say that words like craft and social purpose have long been part of the dialogue of architecture and their presence is expected. Yet, where Architectus' work seems to differ from that of other recent city buildings is the way in which those values are given new importance. What might be seen as the old values of modernism are again given voice in the works themselves, rather than being part of a purely rhetorical architectural vocabulary. This stance reflects a certain faith in the future of architecture as more than business.

To the casual observer of contemporary architecture much of the pleasure derived from a building comes from the notion of permanence. The notions of craft and permanence as architectural values in an Auckland building can be traced back to the presence of buildings like those that collect on the Auckland University campus or even to the few survivors of an earlier architectural culture. They can also be traced to the heavier, more solid architecture of the South Island, which Architectus both acknowledges as an inspiration and to which they have added with their Christchurch works. Notably both Christchurch and Dunedin are cities that New Zealanders regard as having wonderful buildings, rather than wonderful landscapes.

It is in the way that it's recent Auckland works extend the language of permanence to an Auckland setting that Architectus' long-term significance as a city practice probably lies. Architectus has at this point made a clear stance, signalled a clear sense of direction, one slightly at odds with current Auckland practice. It makes the practice distinctive: it remains to be seen whether it makes the practice influential. But, this is, after all, only a mid-term report.

Douglas Lloyd Jenkins is an architectural and design historian, curator and writer well known to New Zealanders through his weekly design and architecture columns in the 'New Zealand Herald' and as the face of Televison New Zealand's 'Big Art Trip'. Recent architectural writing has examined the works of mid-century architects Rigby Mullan and Richard Toy. He is currently working on a 20th century history of the New Zealand house. Douglas Lloyd Jenkins is an Associate Professor at the UNITEC School of Design.

"…both Christchurch and Dunedin are cities that New Zealanders regard as having wonderful buildings, rather than wonderful landscapes."

Patrick Clifford

AN EDITED VERSION OF A LECTURE
FOR THE UNITEC CONTEMPORARY NEW ZEALAND
ARCHITECTS SERIES
30.05.2001

It's somewhat daunting to confront 'one's life's work' when you feel as if you're just beginning and therefore not quite ready for a retrospective. Having said that, Architectus has completed 14 years in practice and built nearly 200 projects. We've entered numerous competitions – 34 at the last count. I think we've won eight. We've been part of a range of joint ventures and adventures with other firms and we've collaborated with many colleagues and consultants. It is important to say that not all projects are the work of Architectus alone. In particular, we have worked with Cook Hitchcock & Sargisson, who were very generous in helping us get started, and more lately with Athfield Architects, among others.

I think most architectural history tends to deal with the what, the how and the why. I am going to focus primarily on the how. How do three people come together to build a body of work?

The beginnings of Architectus came from an Auckland University student job programme. Rewi Thompson, Michael Thomson, Malcolm Bowes, Tim Nees, and I were all mates. We hung around together and seemed to think the same way about architecture. We were sitting around in the studio one day and were approached by John Williams from the Auckland University Architecture Workshop. John had an idea for a holiday work programme, which we were receptive to. We called ourselves 'The 380 Group' because we were paid $3.80 an hour to do the job. As a result of that programme we ended up buying and doing up a house in Balfour Road, Parnell.

We graduated in 1981 and maintained a desire or intention to work together at some time. In the meantime Mike and Malcolm worked for Cook Hitchcock & Sargisson. I went to Wellington where I worked at the Ministry of Works for a couple of years. While there I did a number of private jobs. A house on the hills above Northland, for an old school friend, was about light and colour and the way in which they meet on surfaces. At that time we really didn't think detailing was much more than bringing pieces of gib board together. Programmatically it's very simple and formally it's very simple. It was clad in rusticated weather boards, which at the time seemed pretty sensible because the two adjacent houses were also clad in rusticated weather boards. However, the first day it rained horizontally (as it was going to do reasonably frequently), and the house leaked like a sieve. Water came in between the laps of the weatherboards. We discovered afterwards that the boards weren't machined correctly. The first building, the first disaster.

010
Balfour Road House, Parnell, Auckland
Malcolm Bowes, Rewi Thompson, Tim Nees

Malcolm, Mike and I ended up travelling in Europe, both together and separately. Much of the time was spent visiting and studying buildings, armed with a copy of Peter Murray's *The History of Renaissance Architecture* and a couple of other texts. We obviously visited contemporary works but I really felt, on leaving architecture school, that there was a huge gap in my education in respect of the history of architecture. If there's anything that sticks in my mind about the experience of being overseas, not just from the point of view of visiting buildings but also from working there, was that I began to understand some sense of precedent, architectural precedent. I realised that you could actually study architecture. Up until that point I thought it was born of inspiration that came down to one from above. I grew to feel that it's fundamentally important to look at precedents – to study them and to utilise them. In London I was fortunate to work for an architect who had been educated by Louis Kahn – Ihan Zeybekcoglu. This had a very significant influence on my own thoughts. Until this experience I had never encountered a passion for the plan – the notion of the plan as a kind of stamp, the volumes extruded from it. It really made me realise there were ways of approaching projects other than this kind of architecture of inspiration. Not that one stopped being inspired of course, but I realised that it was possible to feed into a body of pre-existing architecture – into the experiences of other projects.

Malcolm and I worked for Ihan, while Mike was in Terry Farrell's office, a very significant London studio. In 1986 we decided to return to New Zealand and start our own practice. In the early days Cook Hitchcock & Sargisson referred clients to us, and we worked with them on a number of projects. It's quite a revelation to realise how important our peers would be in our careers. The first project we got on our own (a house in Karaka, south of Auckland) was not particularly memorable but it represented some of the values that we would develop as we went along. We thought the project should be disciplined and relatively rigorous but simply organised and sit strongly in the landscape. A lot of what we experienced in New Zealand up to this time was very additive and

021

"Until this experience I had never encountered a passion for the plan – the notion of the plan as a kind of stamp, the volumes extruded from it"

020
House on the hills above Wellington

021
House at Karaka

formal. There was a lot of concern with making shapes, and many of them. We began to think that perhaps there were other ways of doing things.

030 Not that everything was approached so seriously – another early project we
031 did is the Smith House. The client asked us to join together two Japanesesque flats or townhouses on the North Shore, and make one dwelling. It was, I suppose, a quintessential Eighties project. The two previously faux-Japanese townhouses were encapsulated in faux plaster façades. Charles Moore gave us the answer – his blue/grey bow-fronted Rhodes House with the orange groove in front. We simply took its façade and stuck it on the front.

At this time it's fair to say that we were really working somewhat separately. The practice was just the three of us. We'd get a job and talk about it, work initially on it together, then, as the jobs were quite small, one of us would take it on and do it alone.

032 A house in Clive Road, Epsom, Auckland, summarises, in a way, the challenge
033 of houses as we saw them. I remember David Mitchell at the Auckland School of Architecture saying something like, "when you start working just try to get something built, because someone will like it." The risk is you'll build something and they will like it, but it will be something you didn't really want to do. I think with houses people are concerned with the image, with the nature of the expression of the work. As a young architect, before you've built anything, that's quite difficult to deal with. I remember going to visit this site with Mike. We said, look, this is the sort of place that we could build a couple of Meieresque pavilions, connected together. The clients said, hmm, not so sure about that, and came back with a rough plan and an image of how the house

should be. The built result addresses some issues of light and form and some planning issues but it doesn't begin to find what we thought would be an appropriate expression. I suppose it made us understand the difficulty of houses, even though they are the things you tend to do when you start. Clients perhaps engage young architects because they have no body of work, so they think they are able to provide the ingredients and therefore have more direct input. They think it's like ordering a cake: here are the ingredients, now you just bake it for me. Concurrent with this early house we worked on

030 / 031
Smith House, North Shore, Auckland

032 / 033
House at Clive Road, Epsom, Auckland

040 numerous house alterations, including a house at Karaka Bay. We were pretty interested in how you might draw things and represent them, and the influence of Charles Moore is obvious. Mike had brought with him a really clear and extensive understanding of how to build. Around this time we realised that if we joined our respective skills together we could begin to produce better projects.

The same client that engaged us for the house in Clive Road asked us to do
041 another house in Bridgewater Road, Parnell. We began to think of a way of
042 building related to our vicarious experience of Louis Kahn. The extrusion of the plan, the creation of volumes and a more compositional approach. There was a sense of repetition and rhythm appearing in the work. We also realised the image issue was less dominant if the project was built around an interest or idea of the owner. In the Bridgewater Road house, the idea was that of structure – the client being an engineer. There is a shear tower and other pieces of the building are cantilevered or stretched away from that. The floors are a system of very lightweight steel truss with 60mm of concrete on top. The approach and the systems used are more commonly found in commercial construction.

043 Later we did a little office building for the same client. A very simple programme with similarly simple construction – block-walls, round columns, projecting balconies, and a roof light. Obviously in the manner of Mario Botta. The circular element is a screen. We learnt from then on to make everything integrated and essential – card-house-like – so the project could not be marooned by deletion. The screen did not get built.

044 In 1987 we received the commission for a small office on the Tamaki River, east Auckland. The two-level structure is organised around a bar of services and a stair. The upper level pierces and overhangs the larger, skinnier lower level. A series of vaulted roofs is evidence of considered precedents as well as fashion – vaults were everywhere. While this building is quite transparent, we also began to see that buildings could have more specific relationships to their orientation. In this case, the back is closed, the front open. In some of our earlier projects the building is simply 'in the round'. There is a kind of consistency and evenness in the way the project is made.

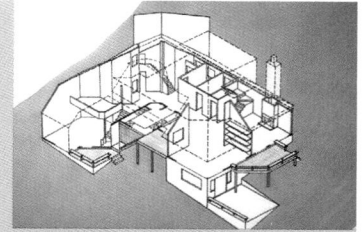

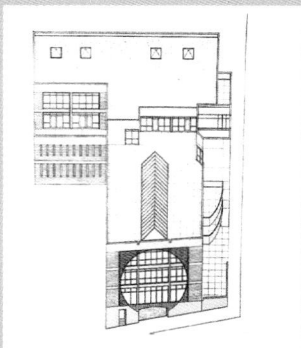

043
Office Building, Newton

044
Office on the Tamaki River

040
House at Karaka Bay

041 / 042
House at Bridgewater Road

050 The Grace House, Mt Eden, was commissioned in 1989 for a lady in her seventies, a great person. The site is cross-leased. The good thing about cross-leases is that you can build right up to the boundary. We made a two-storey piece, screened from existing dwellings, and a single-storey volume, which lies along the cross-lease boundary. It formed a garden wall to the neighbour's property. We believed the garden would grow and just a little roof would be visible. It was in this project that I think we discovered, or rediscovered, Vernon Brown. I am not suggesting that this project is in any way finely related to his work, but it draws on the spirit of his simple forms –

coated in creosote or painted white when cut away to form porches. This house also represents our first serious engagement with detailing. We were able to document the building properly and had a fantastic builder, a great craftsman, who made a beautiful job of it. It really inspired us to engage with the notion of craft. We've since become incredibly interested, some might say, obsessed, with the way things are made and the qualities, which they can have by the way you make them.

051 At the same time we won a competition for the fountain at the Aotea Centre,
052 Auckland. The brief was to represent the way water acts and interacts with the New Zealand landscape. Hence the project is smooth and eroded, tranquil and vigorous. The salutary lesson from this exercise is to be careful when you cross into what you might call artwork. We loved the opportunities to work with great materials and water and the process of building it. A technically difficult project, over-complicated in terms of the kind of mechanisms we used, but an important step in learning how to build.

053 We got a job for a house in the Waitakeres for the guy from whom we were
054 purchasing our first computer. I think he got the better end of the deal because the computer cost $10,000 and it only did word processing! But it was important because we made a commitment to get into computers early, which enabled us to make the transition to larger projects.

051 / 052
Aotea Fountain

050
Grace House, Mt Eden

053 / 054
House in the Waitakeres

In 1989 the Museum of New Zealand, Wellington, competition was announced. It was an open competition and after going through a list of international architects whom we might phone up, we decided that we should do it ourselves – in collaboration with Cook Hitchcock & Sargisson, Ross Jenner from the Auckland School of Architecture and John Scott from Hawke's Bay. We'd been working on the project for a little while when John came up with some objects wrapped in newspaper, walked into the office and slammed them down on the table. He unwrapped two sculptures and said: "That's it". It took a little bit of time to work through that one.

060
061
062
063
Following on from the Museum of New Zealand, we did more competitions – the Venice Gateway and the Museum of Scotland, both with Rewi Thompson. Our proposal for the latter sought to create an inversion of the condition that was found within the building we were adding to. We placed some very heavy galleries onto the site and then mounted them with a light steel-frame, which enabled you to walk over and among those heavy stone galleries – rather like scaffolding. The incumbent building had a heavy exterior and very light steel interior structure. So we took those elements and swapped them over. It's a theme that appears in other projects of ours.

In 1991, I purchased a piece of land, as did Malcolm. The house I subsequently built for Leslie Forsyth and myself would carry on from 1991 until the start of building in 1994. Three years of angst and numerous schemes. Every weekend was spent down at the office working on our house. In a way, it was, I suppose, an escape, and a really pleasurable one, to do something for oneself.

Two residential projects followed that refer back to the comments about the Bridgewater Road house. We began to realise that if you looked in the programme you could probably find something that could anchor the design. Most of the people you work with don't have any exotic characteristics; they simply want two bathrooms, three bedrooms and a family room. However, we were looking around for ways in which to expand the brief. In the first house,
064
065
on Great Barrier Island, there were two families who occasionally stayed in the holiday house together. We proposed separating the sleeping accommodation into two little cabins with a living space between. There's a mezzanine and a lower sleeping area and a little bay window repeated at either end. We'd found here a plan form that we would continue to use in other projects – taking the

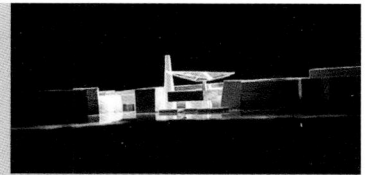

064 / 065
House on Great Barrier Island

060
Venice Gateway

061 / 062 / 063
Museum of Scottland

sleeping accommodation and book-ending it around where you might live. This form allowed the two families to share but equally created space for different family members.

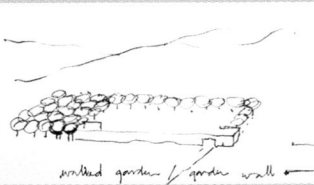

070 Shortly after that we were commissioned to do a project at Te Horo near Wellington. The client's brief was quite detailed but again we figured one could select bits and use them as a kind of armory to create the project. They liked earth bricks and the notion of a walled garden. Influenced by Souta Moura amongst others, we made the project about those two issues – the creation of the house as part of an earth-walled garden. The house has now had thousands of trees planted, forming a great courtyard behind it.

I went off to America in 1994 when my wife was offered a job in New York. I learned to play the harmonica and worked in Michael Sorkin's office. At the
071 same time our house in Kelvin Road was being built in New Zealand, super-
072 vised by Mike. During the year he sent over a packet of slides, which are still favourites of mine in terms of the expression of the building. We'd let the contract only for the shell of the building and it had taken three years to get to that point. It took another year to figure out how to put anything inside it.

At the same time as the house was being finished, we undertook a competition for the University of Canterbury Sciences West Precinct. We'd been included on the competition list, I think, as a result of all the other competitions we'd done. It didn't just happen by chance. We were successful and at the beginning of 1995 we had $30 million of buildings to build at the University –
073 the Mathematics Statistics and Computer Sciences Building and the Sciences
074 Library. It was a real opportunity to develop our thoughts and ideas about services, structure and the social aspects of building. We were influenced, of course, by what we saw and found around us such as the Warren and Mahoney building at Christchurch College, and we loved the opportunity to work in the language of Christchurch. I guess the challenge at this point for a relatively small firm of architects is, having built some quite large buildings, not to go back to being a small firm of architects doing small buildings. However, opportunities of the scale of Canterbury are difficult to find.

We got involved in a couple of high-rise projects in collaboration with Christopher Kelly at Architecture Workshop in Wellington. We invited artist

071 / 072
House at Kelvin Road

073 / 074
MSCS Building

070
House at Te Horo, Market Building by Souta Moura, Market Building by Souta Moura, House at Te Horo

Billy Apple to collaborate with us on the first project, exploring the idea of building as artwork. The second was commissioned by Wellington City to look at an alternative to demolishing three existing structures on Lambton Quay. In 1996, for Housing New Zealand, we were successful in a competition at Rowena Crescent, Glen Innes, Auckland, to add additional houses to an established neighbourhood. Existing houses were moved around and new service lanes formed, allowing dual access to new terrace houses inserted along the street edge.

In 1997 we fitted out an old warehouse and moved the office to Centre Street. We had an Irish guy, Jerry, working with us at the time and he got the 'hospital pass' of doing the office. I think it nearly drove him mad. He had three different people in his ear asking what was going on or offering advice.

In 1999 John Sinclair joined our office and increasingly we found ourselves doing larger commercial and public buildings. This was partially intentional and partially organic. What it meant was a new direction in the type of projects we undertook. The Canterbury University buildings were closely followed by the Jade Stadium job, done in conjunction with Athfield Architects. The New Lynn Community Centre, St Peter's College and Auckland Grammar in Epsom, and the University of Auckland's Tamaki campus extended us further into the realm of civic buildings. You could say the conversion from a residential-based practice into the broader field of larger buildings was complete.

Therefore, having stated at the beginning that it hardly felt the time has come for a retrospective, it is probably appropriate that this be regarded as an interim report. At the end of 2001 Architectus: Bowes Clifford Thomson evolved into an Australasian entity by joining with three Australian practices to form Architectus Auckland, along with Architectus Sydney, Melbourne and Brisbane.

080 / 081
Rowena Crescent

083
New Lynn Community Centre

082
Office, Centre Street

084
St Peter's College Technology Building

Site photomontage

Te Papa Tongarewa

MUSEUM OF NEW ZEALAND
WELLINGTON
COLLABORATION WITH COOK HITCHCOCK
& SARGISSON, ROSS JENNER, JOHN SCOTT
COMPETITION 1989

New Zealand emerged from the ocean thousands of years ago, sliding and thrusting upwards as a result of gigantic ground movements caused by the meeting of two tectonic plates. The Wellington region provides a striking example of these powerful forces of nature.

Maori mythology refers to these events in the story of Maui, who hauled the land from the ocean like a fish from the sea. This is also an account of the concept of emergence, the creation of the world through the chasm produced by the splitting of sky and earth, Rangi and Papa, from which emerged night, sky, seeking, questing, searching, void, the earth, bright day, the world of light. This emergence and uplifting is represented in the building's design by immense tilted floor planes that form the building's base.

The building posed the question of what grounds the ground? How a national, bi-cultural museum is conceived is based not on a fixed hierarchy but presented in an active process of formation, constructed of interweaving, sliding and overlapping, maintaining differences without seeking to fix an essential identity to each race and culture. As a national museum it had to interpret the land without any presupposition of nationhood.

The seaward incline forms an east-west ceremonial processional route from the sea and Marae Atea to the Ahurewa/ Wharenui. The Marae establishes a Maori presence in the city, yet still expresses the relationship of Maori and nature. A bridge connects the Marae and the museum's Maori collection, ensuring the building is constantly enriched by ceremonies. The eastern entry is animated by openness to arrivals from the sea; canoes could land in sheltered waters and be drawn up and stored on the incline.

The incline from the northwest to southeast rises from the square, orienting the building to key city institutions and forming the main public entry. A disc-like level platform is sited at a pivotal intersection between the planes, forming the entry and orientation point to all main public areas. The auditorium, educational areas and public service areas are located directly adjacent, on and under the ground plane.

The design didn't want the complex to be an isolated monument detached from the city, with its back to it. Galleries and related service areas, therefore, form an urban edge, containing conservation and curatorial activities while the collections are set into the rising ground plane.

The gallery ceilings become a constant orientation element, with composition variations and light-control devices characterising each collection as an identifiable container or treasure chest, directly linked to exhibition preparation, conservation and curatorial areas. The principal floor of each is at the level of the incline from where one rises or descends to other floors or crosses between different collections.

Ross Jenner, Architect

Concept sketch

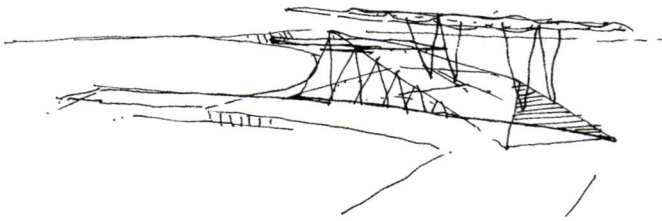

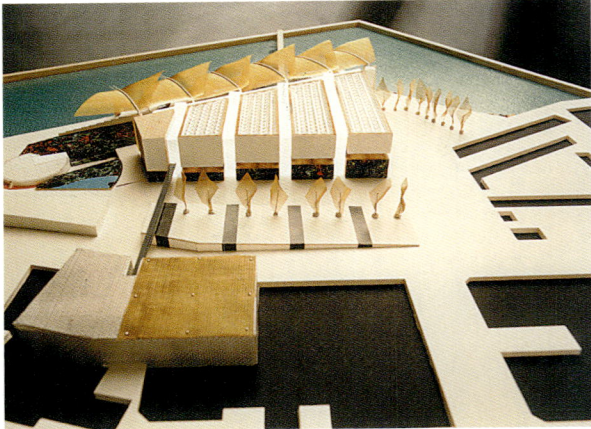

| View from city | View from water | Plan view |

Site photomontage

TEMPORARY EXHIBITIONS GALLERY   COLLECTIONS

MARAE - ATEA   CAFETERIA   RESTAURANT   AHUREWA / WHARENUI

POSSIBLE CONCESSIONS

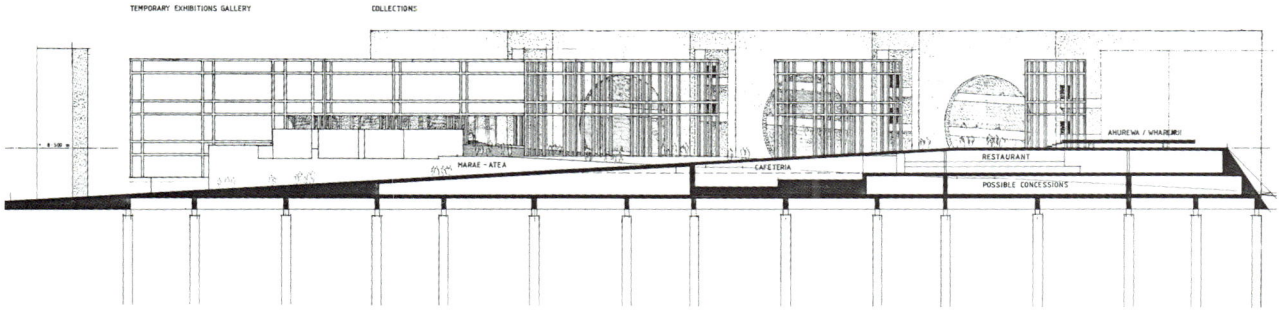

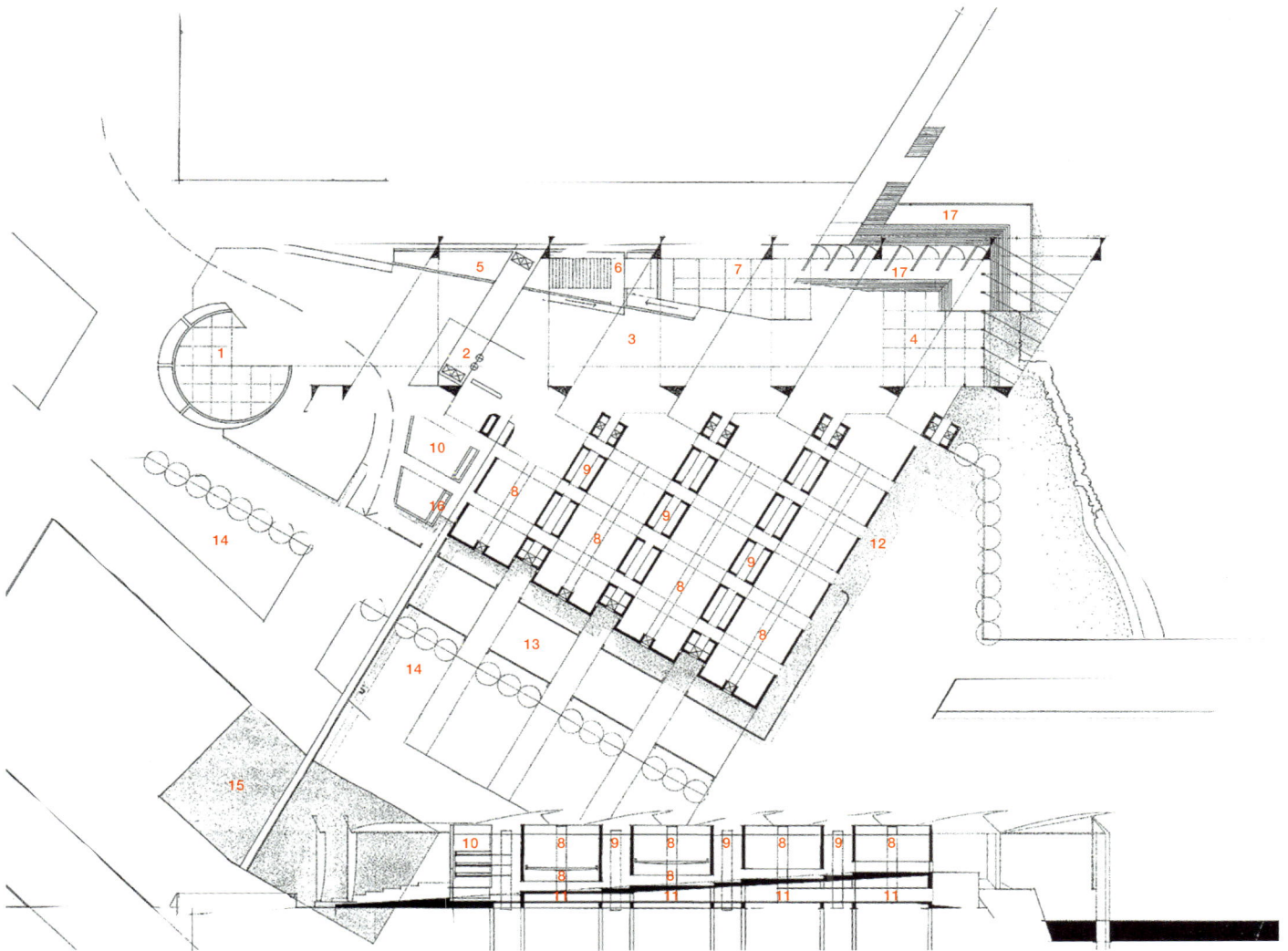

Section through
reception hall

Main floor plan across
rising levels

Section through galleries

1. Place to stand
2. Visitor entrance
3. Reception hall, Marae
4. Ahurewa, Wharenui
5. Visitor orientation
6. Auditorium, public education
7. Refreshments
8. Public exhibition galleries
9. Public research

10. Administration, management
11. Collection storage, central services
12. Service entry
13. Coach, visitor parking
14. Park, future expansion
15. Parking
16. Administration entry
17. Terraces

View from south-east

Clifford Forsyth House

ORAKEI, AUCKLAND
1991 – 1995

This house sits near the Orakei Basin, a tidal waterway connecting to Auckland's harbour. Fingers of land run out from main ridgelines, separated by valleys that fall gradually to the coast, filling with rainfall and seawater as they go. The design concept begins with an investigation of the relationship between a light wooden frame and solid retaining block walls, and an ideal of creating the spirit of a boathouse, a place to retreat to, almost a holiday house within the city.

The primary elements of construction, frame and walls, sit on a concrete base, while a folded plate roof, underlined with plywood, tops the whole. Block-work elements, which began life as a core (enclosing some functions or forming a hearth) are separated, interacting with the frame to divide the space; cupping each end of a 'servant' zone (on the angle of the roof's fold) and compressing the middle of a 'served' zone. Approached from the street above, the house addresses the public edge with a primary, glazed screen stretched between block walls – inclined warmly and welcomingly to the visitor, with an expressed colonnade.

"The formality: the simple, strong geometric basis, structural clarity and even the combination of simple unadorned materials (concrete block, timber and glass) recall Kahn. But while Kahn usually avoided overall symmetry in his houses, Architectus delight in the balanced purity of this structure. Purity is more than visual formalism: it conceals a great density of use, privacy, view and climate."

Rory Spence *The Architectural Review, February 2000*

Wooden shields shelter the western aspect from harsh summer sun, and provide privacy, with strips of louvres spanning back to the primary elements. Two-storey joinery walls connect to the frame at either end – mostly solid at the south, glazed to the north with adjustable shutters to sleeping areas. Cabinetry, painted white and detailed neutrally, contrasts with the natural, grainy finish of the container, defining simple space divisions – bedrooms, bathroom, kitchen.

"The house is not merely well done; it corresponds to my own taste. The sources? Eames, perhaps Aalto, a certain antipodean lightness that comes of the logical economies of the new. There's a balance to this house that shows both a certainty and a courtesy towards its setting in both culture and nature. I like this differential elegance very, very much and – looking at the photos, thinking of Patrick, delightful image of breezy nights abed by the open window, of gin and tonics on the terrace listening to the clink of ice cubes and glasses and the rustle of the creek as it descends to the sea. And, at night, I can imagine the place glowing like a lantern."

Michael Sorkin UME 4

Site plan

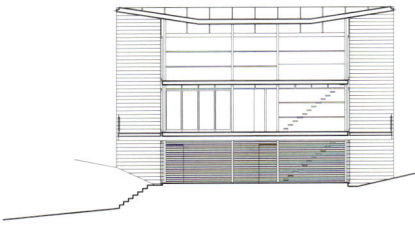

Living area

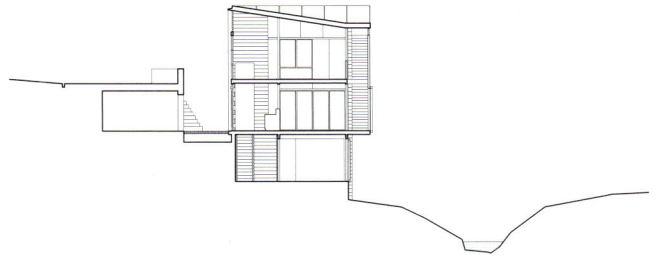

View from south-west

View from east

Living area, looking north

View from north

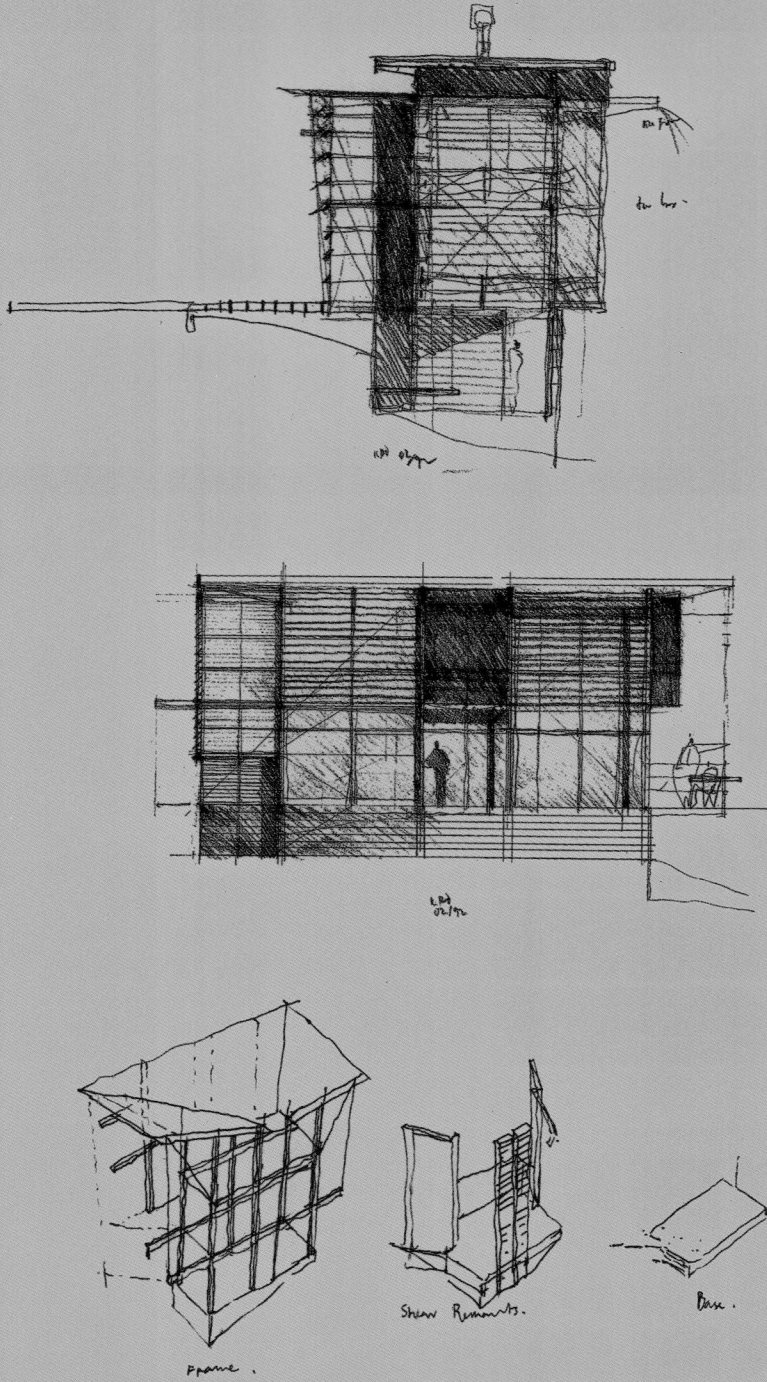

Elevation sketches

Diagram showing
structure

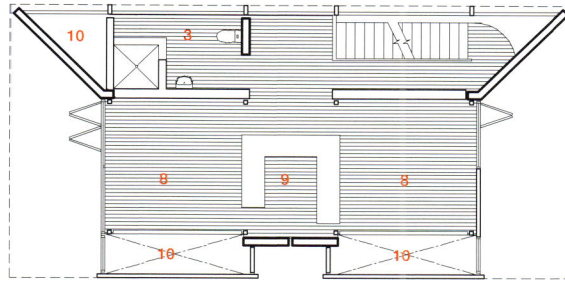

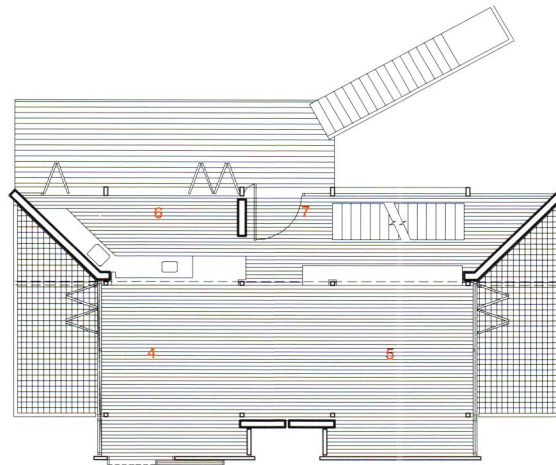

Floor plans:

Level 3

Level 2

Level 1

1. Family
2. Store
3. Bathroom
4. Dining
5. Living
6. Kitchen
7. Entry
8. Bedroom
9. Dressing
10. Void

Sectional model showing circulation
and bookcase spine

Sciences Library

SCIENCES WEST PRECINCT,
UNIVERSITY OF CANTERBURY
CHRISTCHURCH
COLLABORATION WITH COOK HITCHCOCK
& SARGISSON/ROYAL ASSOCIATES
COMPETITION 1994

In 1994 the University of Canterbury held an invited design competition for a Sciences Precinct at its Ilam campus. The competition called for the design of the precinct master plan and two buildings: a building for the Mathematics Statistics and Computer Sciences departments and a Sciences Library. Each could have been awarded to separate architects. In the event, the submission by Architectus was successful for all three parts.

"It was decided the competition should include both a precinct development plan and the building sketch designs. With hindsight, this proved a sound move, with the emergence of a single precinct development concept, which was clearly superior in regard to the workability and amenity within the two proposed buildings, the formation of open spaces within the precinct, and the impact of development upon adjacent areas of the campus.

This concept involved the positioning of the Mathematics Statistics and Computer Science building along the southern edge of the precinct with service access from the roadway along this boundary. An open space between this building and the existing Physical Sciences Library mirrored the retention of a further open space to the north, permitting the pavilion-like form and character of the existing library to be retained. The new Sciences Library was positioned along the western boundary of the precinct to define a four-storey edge between academic and service sectors of the campus and to contain (this) open space.

The Architectus submission was distinctive for its close analysis of the University's brief and the insightful interpretation of this brief in relation to the opportunities and constraints presented by this part of the campus. This analysis informed the architectural scheme or parti for both buildings and this parti has been vigorously developed into an architecture with clear tectonic properties and an architectural language sympathetic to the earlier campus architecture.

The library has been shaped as much by precinct objectives as by functional ones – made possible by large areas of functionally undifferentiated floor space. The major part of this building borders the western edge of the precinct, with a mainly closed façade onto the maintenance workshops also limiting the entry of western sun. A deep timber screen wall containing services and individual study carrels provides a longitudinal organizing element of the plan at each floor level, with interfloor stairs rising through the void on the eastern side of this spine. In their design report the architects observe that as the library's books gradually disappear (with the move to electronic information retrieval) this vestigial bookcase would hold that memory. A glazed eastern wall allows those occupying this space to look into the precinct and, conversely, those outside and in the Physics/Chemistry building opposite to observe activities within the library."

John Hunt Architecture New Zealand, September/October 1995

The Sciences Library was taken to documentation stage but has yet to be constructed.

Model showing Sciences Library in context with Mathematics Statistics and Computer Sciences Building

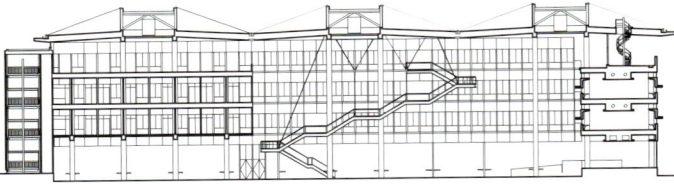

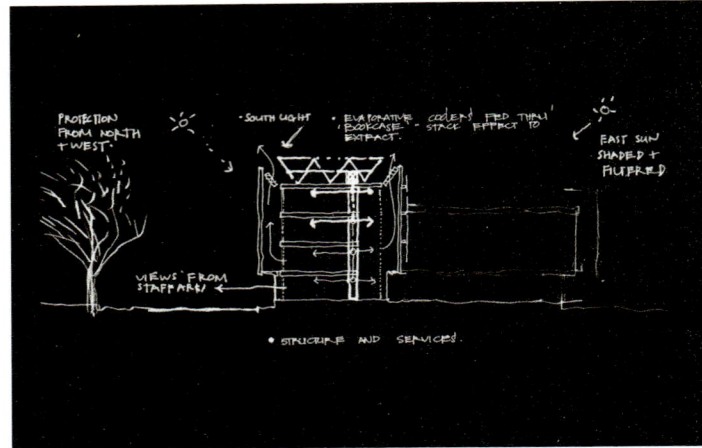

Perspective

Concept sketch

View from south with existing
Physical Sciences Library

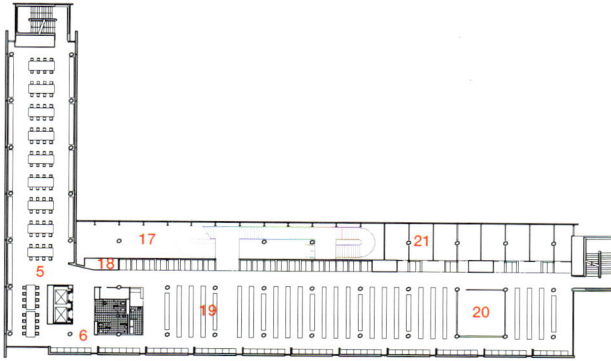

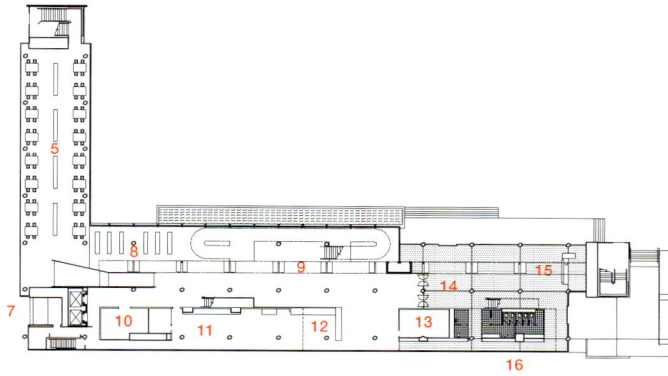

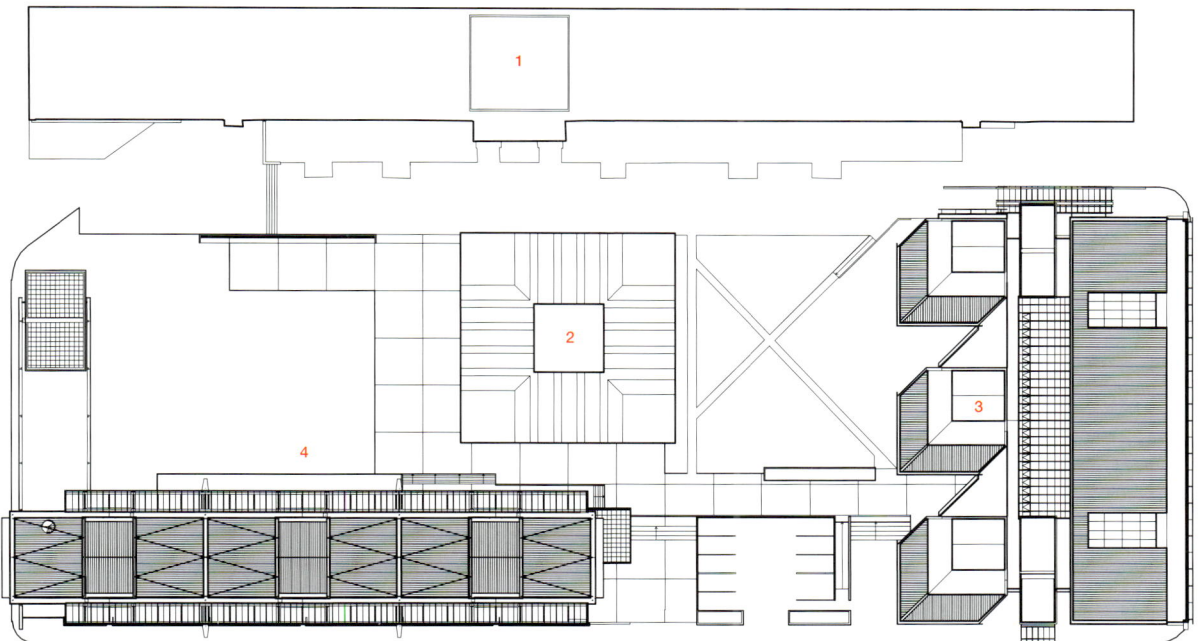

Floor plans:

Level 3

Level 1

Site plan

1. Existing Physics and Chemistry Building
2. Existing Physical Sciences Library
3. Mathematics Statistics and Computer Sciences Building
4. Sciences Library
5. Reading spaces
6. Perimeter seating
7. Cart dock
8. Reference/3 day loan
9. Catalogues
10. Photocopy room
11. Staff workroom
12. Information/circulation desk
13. Audiovisual room
14. Entry lobby
15. Student facilities
16. Toilets
17. Void
18. Carrells
19. Bookstacks
20. Computer room
21. Discussion room

View of the academic
towers in context, angled
north to catch the sun

Mathematics Statistics and Computer Sciences Building

SCIENCES WEST PRECINCT,
UNIVERSITY OF CANTERBURY,
CHRISTCHURCH
COLLABORATION WITH COOK HITCHCOCK
& SARGISSON/ROYAL ASSOCIATES
1994 – 1998

Positioned perpendicular to the existing Physics and Chemistry Building, the MSCS Building forms the southern perimeter of the Sciences West Precinct, and a courtyard bounded by the Physical Sciences Library to the north. It also draws on the materials and construction form of much of the original campus, developed in the 1960s in a mostly Modernist or Brutalist manner.

Conceptually the building is divided into two distinct zones of learning – the three (seven-storey) academic towers for staff and postgraduate research, and the four-storey teaching wing for under-graduate studies. These two elements are brought together around a top-lit atrium, contained on its remaining two sides by vertical circulation/service cores.

The academic offices within the towers are arranged in north facing 'clusters', enjoying views across the plains to the Southern Alps. The offices, naturally ventilated with manually operated mechanisms controlling both sun and ventilation, depending on the season and time of day, are arranged in groups of 10, clustered around vertically stacked double-height spaces with an intercon-necting stair. These shared spaces, with whiteboard and sometimes a kitchenette, are used for tutorials, coffee breaks and other informal meetings.

Across the atrium, on the opposite side, the teaching block faces south, enjoying natural light and generous views across Okeover lawn, without the problems of glare and solar gain, an important consideration for the computer labs. Three levels lower than the academic towers, the teaching block reduces the apparent bulk and overshadowing effects when viewed from Okeover lawn to the south.

"Architectus' first major building is a very impressive achievement and particularly refreshing after much appalling crass post-modern work of the 1980s, especially in Christchurch, and the skin-deep decon-structive games of recent years. The balance of architectural qualities is particularly striking: the building is simple and clear in its organisation yet remarkably varied in formal, spatial and material character. It is architecturally dramatic and seductive, yet it is also socially responsive to its users (academic staff talk of 'unbelievable response' to their needs by the architects, who seemed to 'read our minds', resulting in a 'brilliant design' – such responses to institutional architecture are all too rare today), adaptable to change and energy conserving.

Finally, the architects' unusually frank acknowledgment of overseas sources is balanced by respect for New Zealand's own traditions and the building's local context."

Rory Spence *Architecture New Zealand September/October 1998*

Detail of clusters

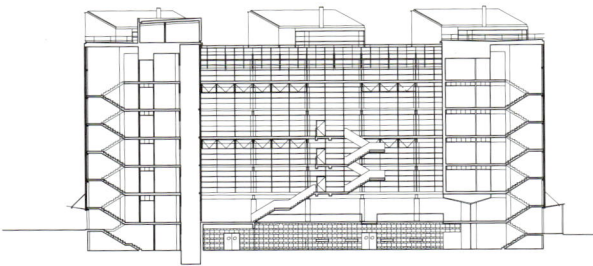

View from the central atrium stair
into the academic towers

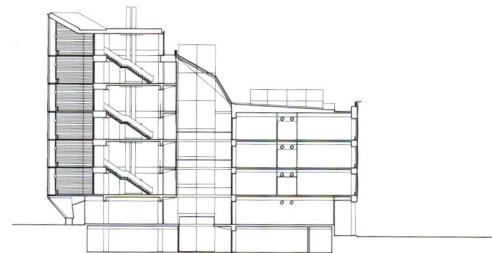

View from the south-west, teaching wing

Double height space – informal study
and research area

View from the north-west,
academic towers, stair tower,
teaching wing

Atrium

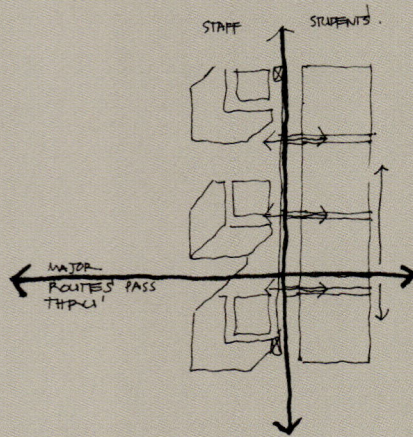

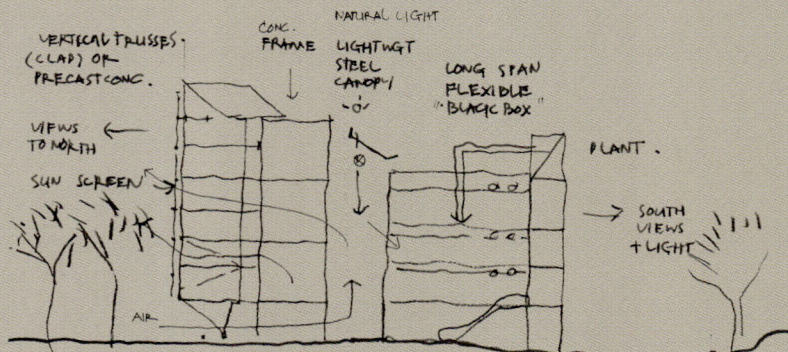

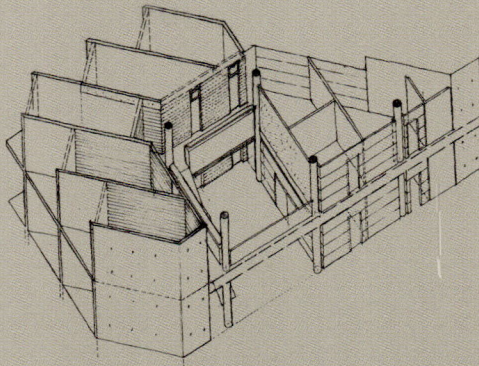

Circulation plan

Diagrammatic section through academic towers, atrium
and teaching wing

Axonometric of part of academic towers showing the
space serving a cluster of offices on two floors

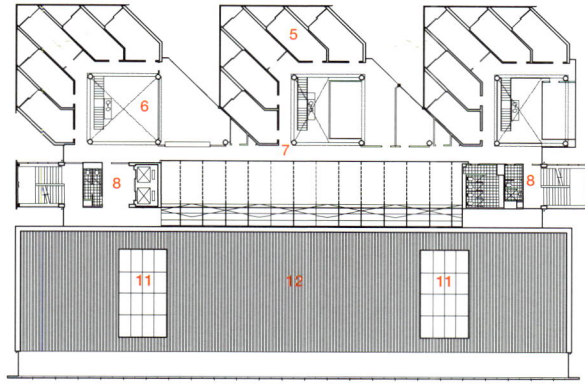

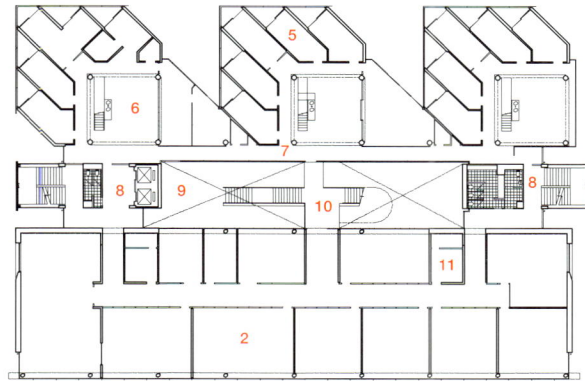

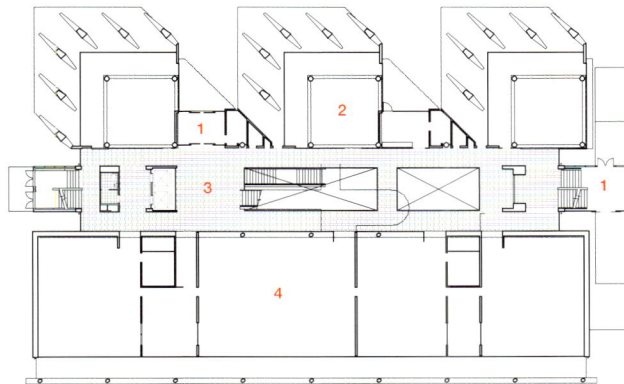

Floor plans:

Level 5
Level 2
Level 1

1. Entrance
2. Tutorial room
3. Concourse
4. Computer lab
5. Academic office
6. Double height space
7. Walkway
8. Core
9. Atrium
10. Bridge
11. Plant
12. Roof

The main concourse with its
ramped approach

Jade Stadium

CHRISTCHURCH
COLLABORATION WITH
ATHFIELD ARCHITECTS/ELLERBE BECKET
1998 – 2002

By its sheer size alone the West Stand commands attention. One hundred metres long and fourty metres high, it is an unmissible presence on the Christchurch skyline, filling the void left two decades ago by the Gas Works. But the building has much more to offer than sheer bulk. Visitors entering the stadium are presented with a series of impressive architectural experiences before they even reach their seats. Access for the public is via two long ramps that stretch out to the north and south street margins of the ground. The crowd is drawn up these ramps to the vast, gently curving plaza five metres above ground level.

The full extent of this space is not immediately apparent, since the curve of the stadium obscures the far ends, but the sense of unbounded space that is suggested is enhanced by the forest of circular columns that rise to meet the tiered roof formed by the stand itself. The effect is somewhat like standing within the half section of a great curving Gothic cathedral, the furthest reaches of which are lost in the gloom. Access to the lower levels of the stand is through a series of entrances placed alongside the radial walls, which carry the principal structural load of the building.

For those with seats on the upper levels the main access is via the centrally located, steel-framed ramp hall which projects beyond the outer line of the main plaza. The 1:8 gradient makes for an easy ascent but the experience itself is far from prosaic. As the ramps turn back on themselves the impression of being caged in a Piranesian prison is reinforced by the steel mesh, which substitutes for the enclosing glass curtain wall a more generous budget might have provided.

Release is achieved first at level 2, where the suite of corporate boxes is located. At level 3 the ramp opens directly into the 100 metre long member's lounge, through which access is gained to the third tier of seats, the commentary box and coach's rooms. The top of the ramp spills into the level 4 concourse which fans out to the left and right, offering spectacular views over the city and beyond to the Port Hills and Southern Alps.

The expressed, neo-Brutalist, structure takes advantage of the technology and skill base of the region but also provides a link with a tradition of Canterbury architecture that emerged in the late 1950s and 1960s. For a region which places strong emphasis on its sporting traditions, these architectural references are entirely appropriate. It is a measure of what has been achieved at Jade Stadium that the West Stand can be confidently placed alongside the major public buildings that were built in Christchurch during the 1970s, Warren and Mahoney's Christchurch Town Hall and Beaven and Hunt's stadium at Queen Elizabeth II Park.

Ian Lochead *Architecture New Zealand, July/August 2002*

Stadium in its Christchurch surroundings with the Port Hills in the background

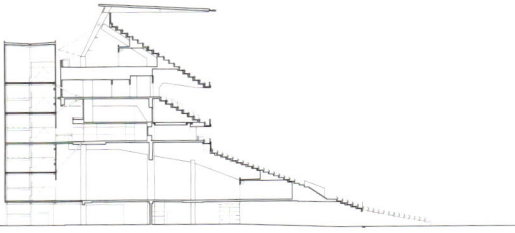

The main concourse

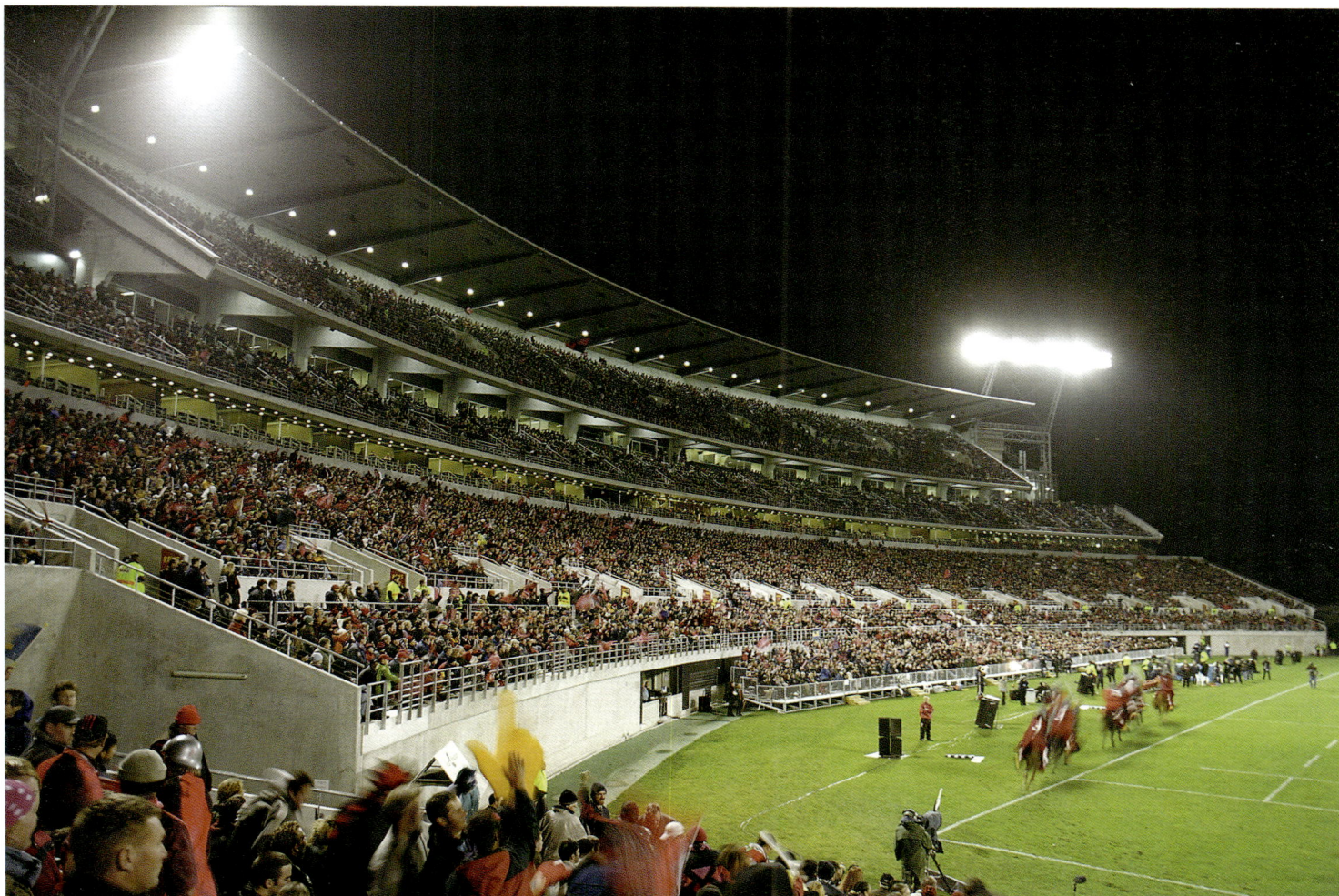

Entry up to the concourse

The west stand: general view of seating bowl

Approach to stadium showing main circulation ramps

CLUB LOUNGE + ↴
SEATS.

SUITES ↴

PUBLIC OVER ↴

+5.0M. ↴

PLAYERS / SERVICE BELOW

PLAYERS BELOW.

PUBLIC OVER (CONCOURSE.)

• PRIMARY MOVEMENT PLAN

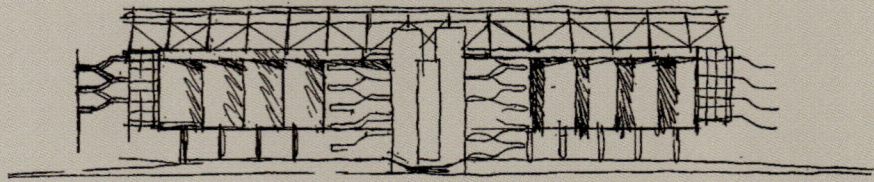

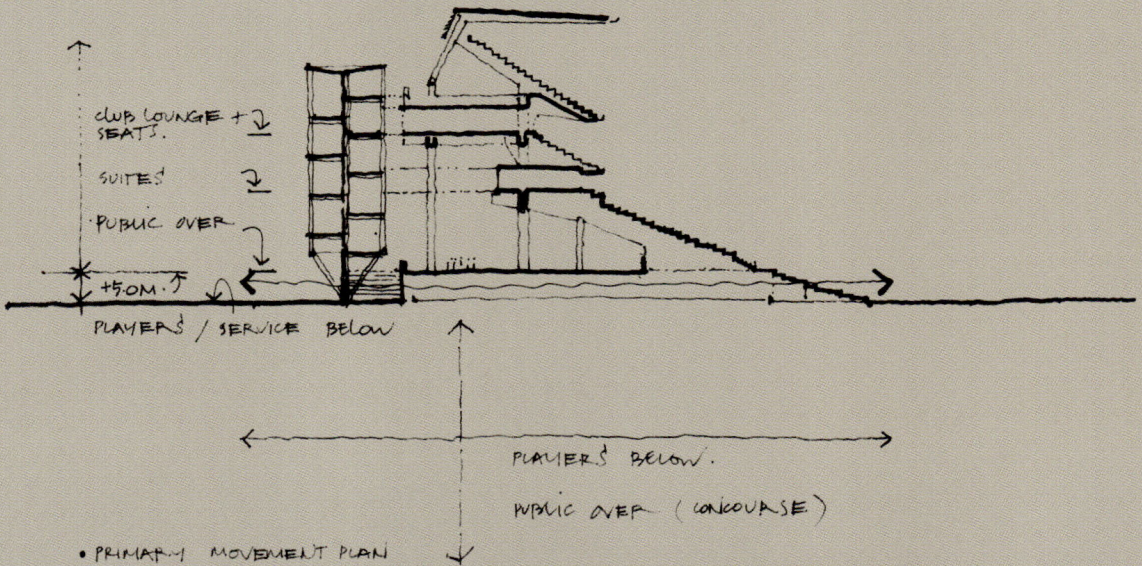

Concept sketches of
elevation and section

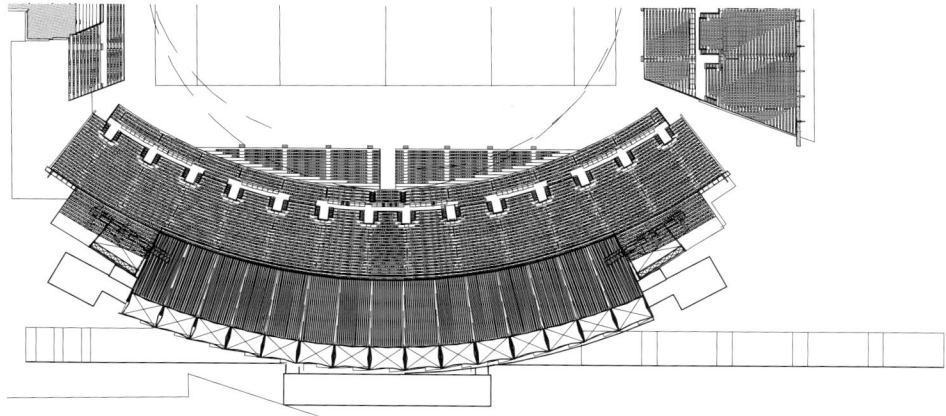

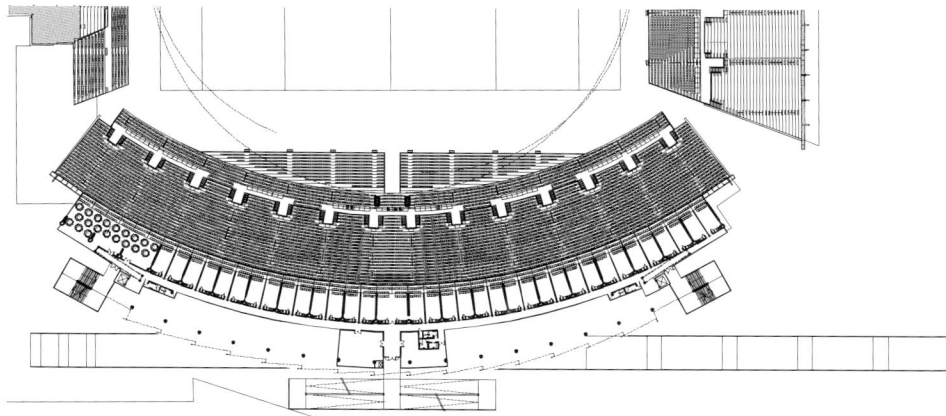

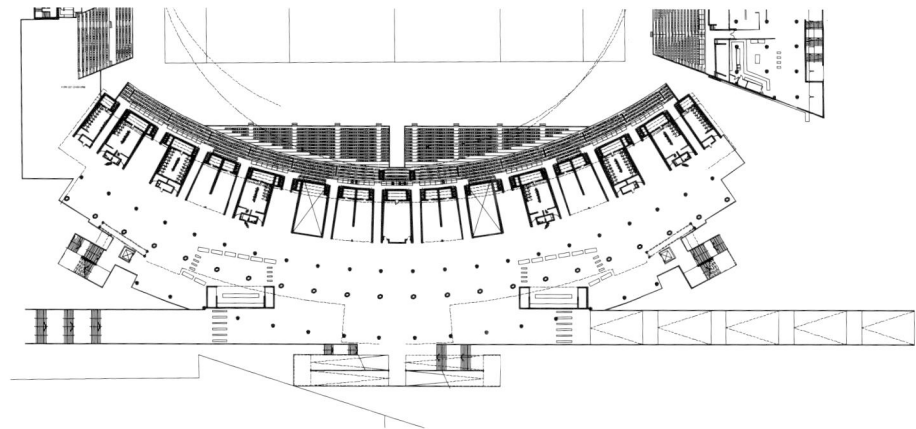

Floor plans:
Upper seating tier
Corporate box level (2)
Concourse level

Elevation to the street

111 Wellesley Street

SALES TECHNOLOGIES OFFICES
AUCKLAND
1999 – 2000

The brief for this project was to convert an existing two-level warehouse in a changing part of the Central Business District into a working environment for a software sales and development company. Typical of this type of conversion, the new use (office) had some demands that differed significantly from those amenities required by the old use (storage). This created both an opportunity and a challenge.

Access to natural light and aspect lay at the core of Architectus' initial investigation for the project. The location, placement and organisation of the service core proceeded in tandem with attempts to optimise the local environment and respond to the client's general organisational requirements (the brief called for a combination of cellular offices and group work spaces, along with meeting spaces, reception, storage, and social areas).

Critical in this investigation was what to do with the space that could not be built, fire egress and accessibility requirements allowed two full upper floors, minus a bit.

The conclusion, agreed with the client (after an options investigation), was to follow a simple courtyard form. This space is positive as an occupiable outdoor room; and negative as a light well, visual connection both vertically and horizontally, and organiser. The new construction was added on top of and around that which exists, recording the changes made. The design endeavoured to allow the new work to aggregate with the old, to add rather than subsume.

"A closer inspection reveals a lot of architecture in this small building. Indeed, in the absence of irony, excess or that retro-modern stylism that trivialises so much current work, one is convinced by its directness and – to use an already overexposed term - transparency.

Perhaps what is really important about this comparatively modest project is that it is a mainstream commercial space, with programme and budget to match. It is not, like the Canterbury building, a product of institutional funding. Neither is it the more-expensive-than-we-let-on kind of detached house that makes up the bulk of published work in New Zealand. Significantly, the architects have resisted the temptation to furnish the client with an 'image', instead concentrating on construction – with modest materials and light – the optimum environmental conditions for work and social interaction between the people using the spaces.

This is the real thing – space, not concept. But made possible by a willingness to conceptually re-engage with the defining limitations of contemporary practice: of time, cost, legislation, human comfort, craft, and the weakness of the profession in relation to the increasingly standardised materials."

Charles Walker *Architecture New Zealand, January/February 2001*

Context

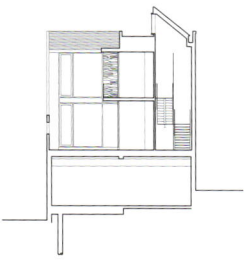

Courtyard

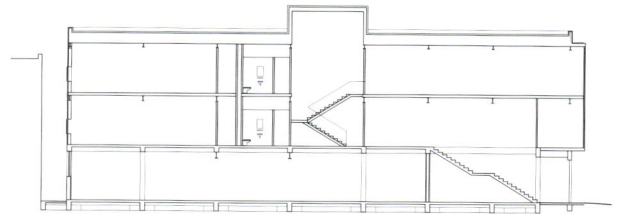

Street façade

View from west showing existing
and new construction

Reception looking through to
conference room

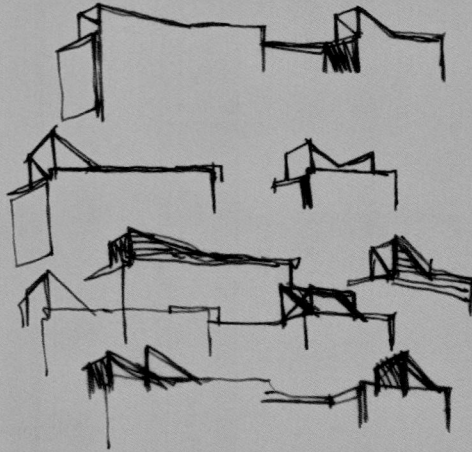

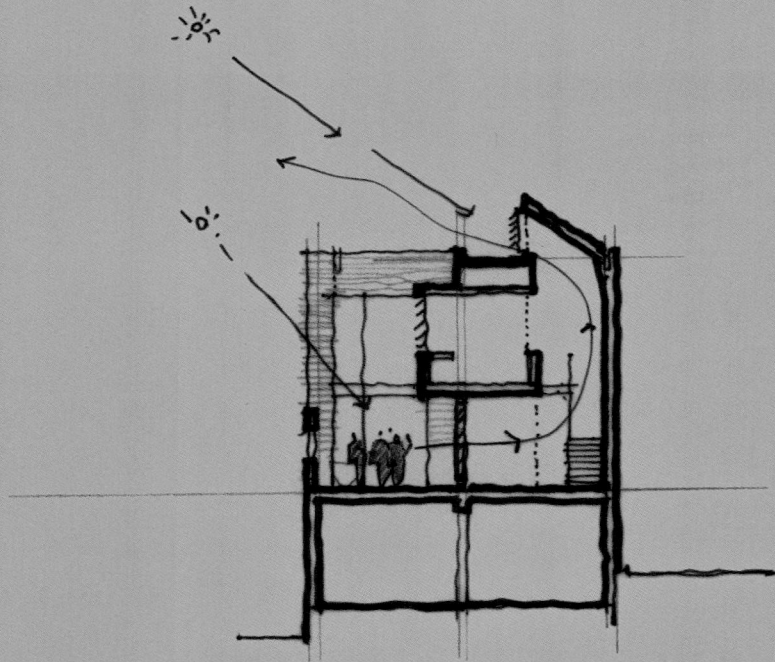

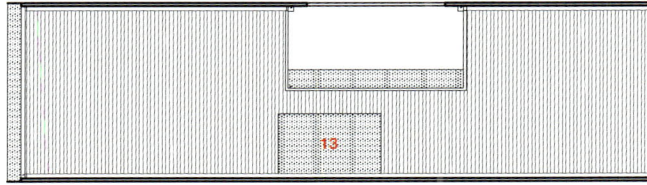

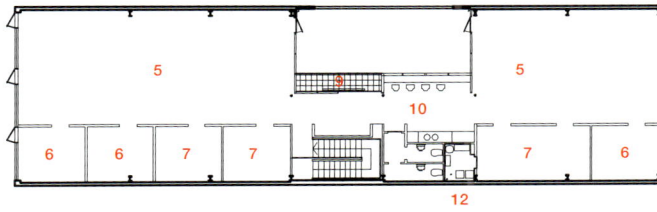

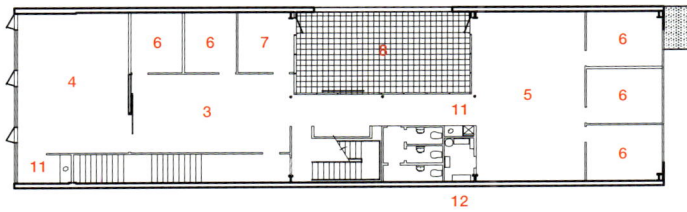

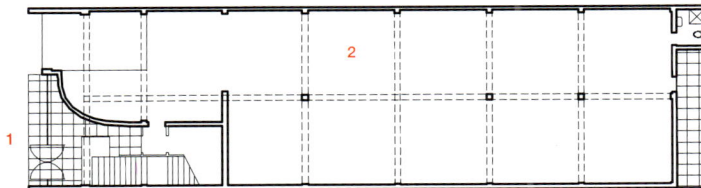

Floor plans:

Roof

Level 3

Level 2

Level 1

1. Entrance
2. Parking
3. Reception
4. Conference
5. Open plan office
6. Office
7. Meeting
8. Courtyard
9. Deck
10. Cafe
11. Kitchenette
12. Plant
13. Skylight

View from north-west

Netball Court-cover

AUCKLAND COLLEGE OF EDUCATION
1999 – 2000

The Auckland College of Education (formerly the Auckland Teachers Training College) is located in the suburb of Epsom, some two kilometres from the city centre.

A former secondary school, the site was developed in the early 1970s. A large number of buildings were constructed, designed by a young team at Architects, Thorpe Cutter Pickmere and Douglas, in the heroic style of Post-Brutalist rationalism – an antipodean expression of the cool, high-tech work of the Smithsons and Archigram in England. Massive structures constructed from lightweight materials to rigorously rational principles, eschewing decoration while trumpeting the expression of their own tectonics. Flat fibrolite sheet, aluminium glasshouse glazing systems, metal roofs, steel beams and laminated timber portals, assembled with skill and the *brio* of youthful idealism.

Since 1996 Architectus has carried out a number of projects on the site, mainly minor alterations and interventions but including larger scale projects, working within the context of tectonic expression and rationalism, approaches inherent in their work, but with a perhaps more restrained aesthetic.

The Netball Court-cover, as its name implies, encloses an existing outdoor 'Astroturf' playing court adjacent to the College's gymnasium. Sharing one wall with the gymnasium, simple steel portals span the court and support a combination of profiled metal and translucent cladding. There are large metal roller doors at each end of the building allowing vehicle access, as well as normal sized hinged access doors, and doors connecting directly to the gymnasium in the shared wall. Internally, the end walls are lined with particle board while the translucent western wall is protected from errant balls by wire mesh. In all, the space enclosed is a rectangle 35 metres by 23 metres by 8 metres high, providing not only an all-weather playing and practice field but also an economical teaching space.

The building's section, both formally and structurally, takes its cue from the existing gymnasium's large, curved and sculpted laminated timber portals. The Court-cover reflects these in shaped steel portals, similar but not the same, while the translucent cladding and galvanised purlins of the western elevation are a simplified version of the aluminium and glass roof glazing of the original building.

Environmental control is simple, basic and effective. Low level timber flaps along the western wall and the large roller doors at the ends of the building can be opened to provide natural cross ventilation. This can be supplemented by high level extract fans if required. Gas heaters are mounted on the shared wall by the teaching area.

The Netball Court-cover extends the language of the existing college buildings not so much out of deference but with respect, welcoming the opportunity to work in a context that reflects Architectus' architectural interests.

Aerial photo showing TSSC Building (upper left) and court-cover in context

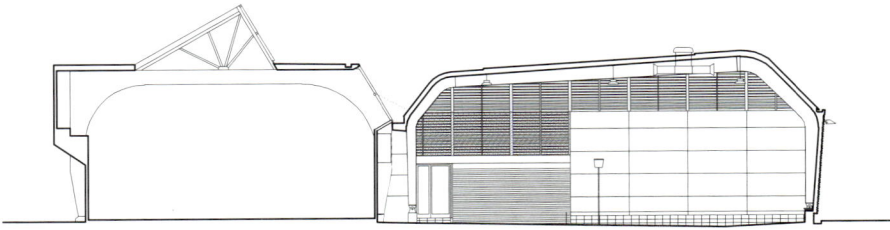

View from south showing
gymnasium beyond

View from west

Interior view

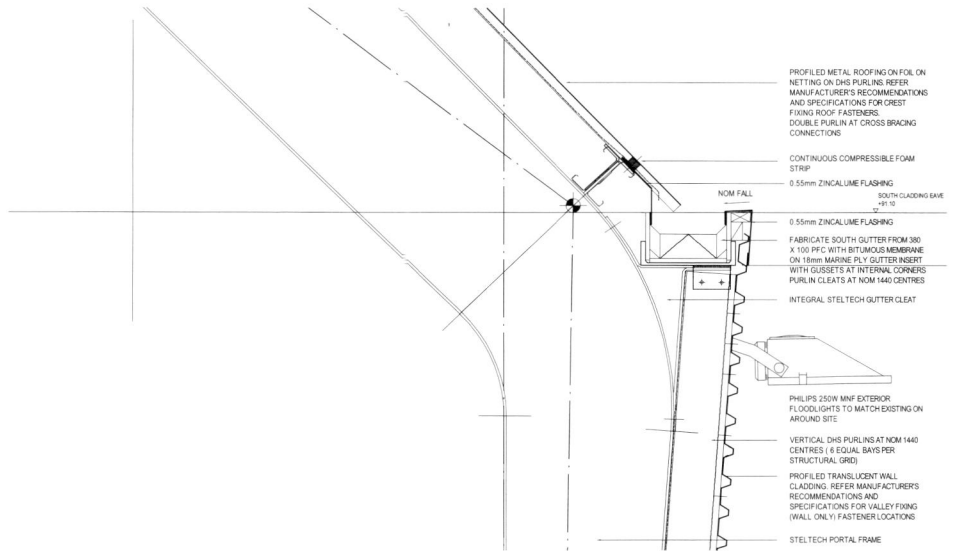

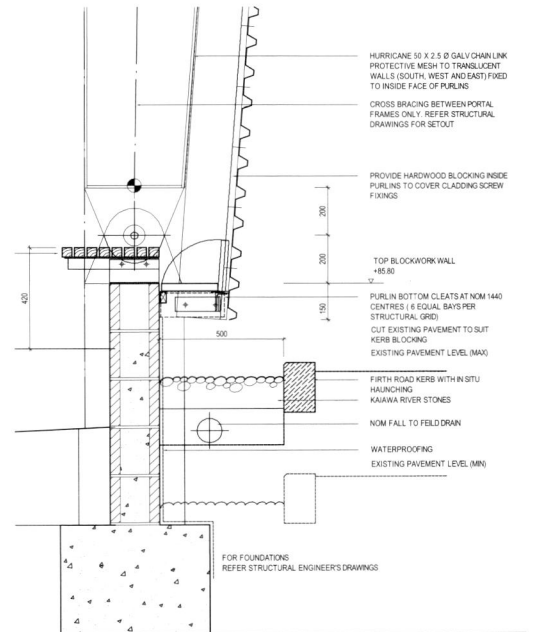

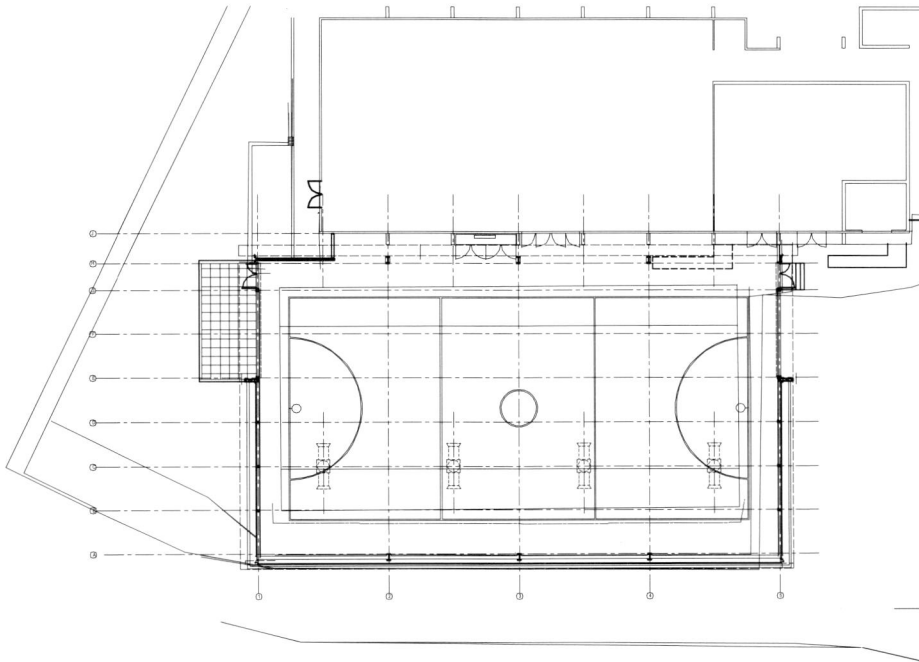

PROFILED METAL ROOFING ON FOIL ON
NETTING ON DHS PURLINS. REFER
MANUFACTURER'S RECOMMENDATIONS
AND SPECIFICATIONS FOR CREST
FIXING ROOF FASTENERS.
DOUBLE PURLIN AT CROSS BRACING
CONNECTIONS

CONTINUOUS COMPRESSIBLE FOAM
STRIP

0.55mm ZINCALUME FLASHING

SOUTH CLADDING EAVE
+91.10

NOM FALL

0.55mm ZINCALUME FLASHING

FABRICATE SOUTH GUTTER FROM 380
X 100 PFC WITH BITUMOUS MEMBRANE
ON 18mm MARINE PLY GUTTER INSERT
WITH GUSSETS AT INTERNAL CORNERS
PURLIN CLEATS AT NOM 1440 CENTRES

INTEGRAL STELTECH GUTTER CLEAT

PHILIPS 250W MNF EXTERIOR
FLOODLIGHTS TO MATCH EXISTING ON
AROUND SITE

VERTICAL DHS PURLINS AT NOM 1440
CENTRES (6 EQUAL BAYS PER
STRUCTURAL GRID)

PROFILED TRANSLUCENT WALL
CLADDING. REFER MANUFACTURER'S
RECOMMENDATIONS AND
SPECIFICATIONS FOR VALLEY FIXING
(WALL ONLY) FASTENER LOCATIONS

STELTECH PORTAL FRAME

HURRICANE 50 X 2.5 Ø GALV CHAIN LINK
PROTECTIVE MESH TO TRANSLUCENT
WALLS (SOUTH, WEST AND EAST) FIXED
TO INSIDE FACE OF PURLINS

CROSS BRACING BETWEEN PORTAL
FRAMES ONLY. REFER STRUCTURAL
DRAWINGS FOR SETOUT

PROVIDE HARDWOOD BLOCKING INSIDE
PURLINS TO COVER CLADDING SCREW
FIXINGS

TOP BLOCKWORK WALL
+85.80

PURLIN BOTTOM CLEATS AT NOM 1440
CENTRES (6 EQUAL BAYS PER
STRUCTURAL GRID)

CUT EXISTING PAVEMENT TO SUIT
KERB BLOCKING

EXISTING PAVEMENT LEVEL (MAX)

FIRTH ROAD KERB WITH IN SITU
HAUNCHING

KAIAWA RIVER STONES

NOM FALL TO FEILD DRAIN

WATERPROOFING

EXISTING PAVEMENT LEVEL (MIN)

FOR FOUNDATIONS
REFER STRUCTURAL ENGINEER'S DRAWINGS

200

200

420

150

500

Floor plan

Section detail

View from south-west
showing advisors' bays

Teacher Support Services Centre

AUCKLAND COLLEGE OF EDUCATION
1999 – 2000

The TSSC building, another addition to the Auckland College of Education, Epsom campus, provides permanent accommodation for the Teacher Support Services – an educational service providing ongoing curriculum support and advice for schools and teachers. The service is supplied by 10 advisor groups of five or so people. Each group specialises in a subject area, supported by administrative staff.

The site for the building is bounded on three sides: to the west by a curving avenue of pohutukawa, to the east by the Kohanga Reo building, and along the northern edge by the Kohia building. The site's primary pedestrian and vehicular entry is from the south.

Positioned perpendicular to the existing Kohia building, the TSSC forms the western perimeter of a courtyard to be strengthened by future redevelopment of the Kohanga Reo site. The entry lobby for the TSSC building forms an internal connection with the Kohia centre. Externally a covered walkway links this lobby space with the campus carpark building, located to the east of the Kohanga Reo.

The building is divided in two, along a north-south axis; to the west the advisors' spaces and to the east, administration. These two elements are brought together around a top-lit atrium terminated at its northern end by the shared lobby space.

The 10 advisors' spaces are arranged in bays spread over two levels. These bays rotate around the atrium following the curvature of the pohutukawa avenue. Each bay is naturally ventilated with various passive mechanisms for additional environmental control, including external sun shading louvres and internal light shelves to bounce natural light back into each space. The bays are designed to accommodate four to five people, with additional space for casual group meetings.

There is a direct response to the fundamental structure of the organization, which allows the development of this somewhat hybrid workspace – not open-plan, not cellular, but grouped.

Across the atrium, in the administration block, the various offices, meeting rooms, services, and staff areas are arranged in a linear fashion along an orthogonal bar. The administration spaces incorporate the same environmental controls as the advisors' spaces.

The circulation zone links the spaces and functions of the project together, encouraging and supporting social interaction in the workplace.

Advisors' space

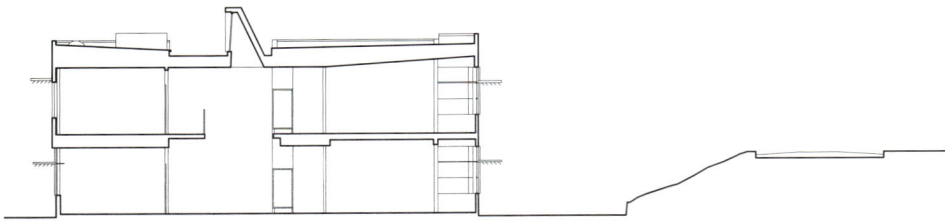

View from east, offices and entry

View from west

Atrium, looking south

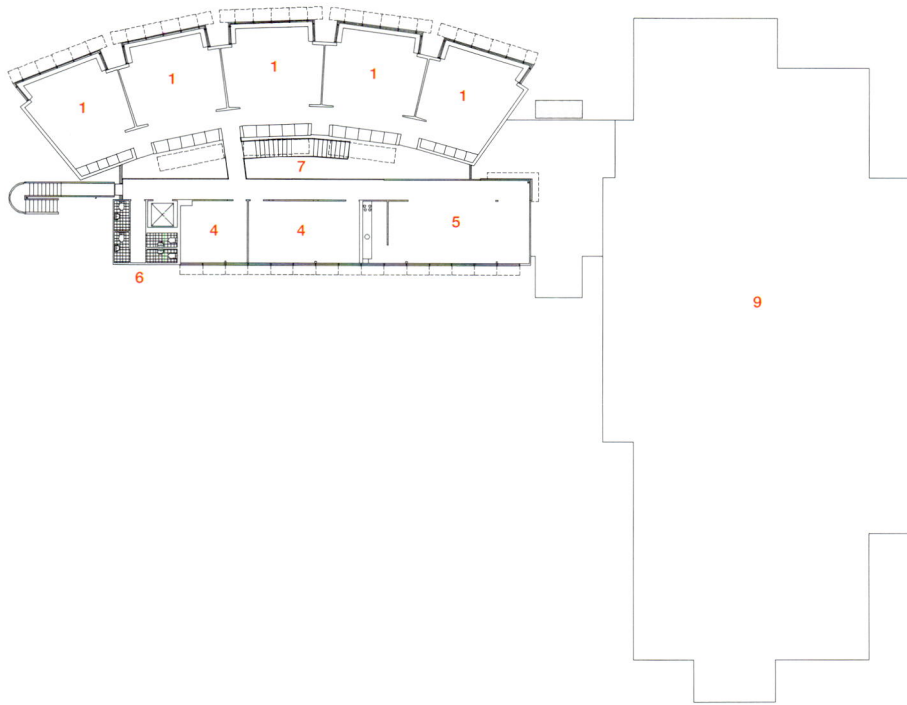

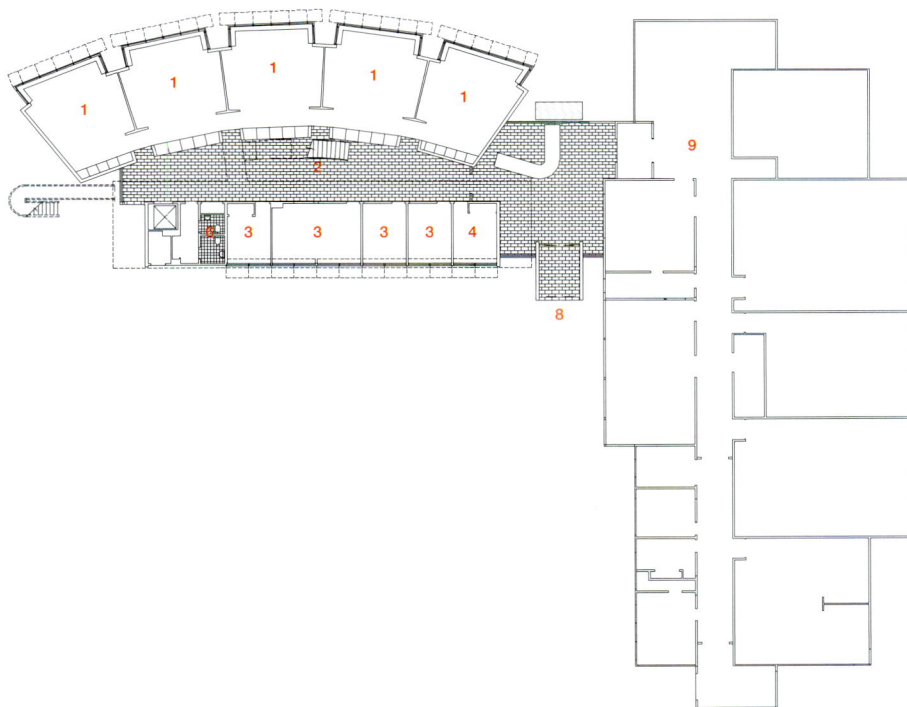

Floor plans:

Level 2

Level 1

1. Advisors' space
2. Atrium
3. Office
4. Meeting
5. Lunchroom
6. Core
7. Void
8. Entry
9. Kohia

View from north

New Technology Building

THE BROTHER L.H. WILKES BUILDING
ST PETER'S COLLEGE
AUCKLAND
1999 – 2001

Before I built a wall I'd ask to know
What I was walling in or walling out
And to whom I was likely to give offence
Robert Frost, *"Mending Wall"*.

For Architectus – who seem to believe in Kahn's unity of "Thought with Feeling" and see the act of building as craft-based métier rather than instrumental technique - the decision as to what to wall in or out seemed clear from an early stage. Resisting the temptation to form a curve, or indeed any other modish form, they have folded a piece of the motorway into a cranked, defensive palisade – forming an apparently effortless integration of architecture and sculpture.

Here the opalescent site-specific installation protectively embraces a series of generic rooms – flexible, decent sized workshops-cum-labs-cum-studio, arranged orthogonally on two levels to form one side of a new shared courtyard and linked by cloister, open stair and bridge to adjacent buildings.

Where possible, internal partitions are transparent to allow supervision between spaces. External or covered circulation places allow for informal gathering and communication, creating "spaces of no obligation' as offerings to students. The narrow site would have prevented putting service spaces on the motorway side so they have been moved to the ends, bookending the "spaces for concentration".

So far, so Architectus. Their previous buildings have been characterized by a straightforward, more or less orthogonal, formal and programmatic didacticism. Here, the box is cut open, forming what the Architects call a hinge. And, possibly, an architectural turning point for the practice itself. While the heavy, hovering wall remains within a traditional parti – set apart and invested with symbolic importance yet symbiotically dependent on its associated architectonic frame – form and programme are separated (granted, not by much), the former no longer seeking to express, but instead loosely accommodating the latter.

Inside the courtyard the grand gesture gives way to a series of relaxed but subtle spatial devices. The detached cut-out planes are more Venturi than Kahn, the cloister more Kresge than Kings College. The effect of the whole is to suggest moments of subtle definition and re-direction – discreet episodes rather than grand narrative.

Nevertheless it is on the motorway side that this secular oratory will inevitably be judged. Part billboard, part illuminated icon, part ribboned gift-box, part lampshade, it also serves to set St Peter's apart from its stylistically similar competitor up the hill. Constructed with an almost painterly eye for composition, the building's assurance and presence underlines architecture's claim to public art.

The still, contemplative luminous cross becoming blurred by movement engages as much as, if not more, than any work by Ito, Gerhard Richter, Uta Barth, Bill Culbert or Ralph Hotere. So what if there are only store-rooms behind the cross? In this context their mystery and inaccessibility becomes all the more compelling. They may also subtly realize Kahn's dictum that a truly great building needs bad spaces as well as good spaces.

Charles Walker *Architecture New Zealand November/December 2001*

In context beside motorway

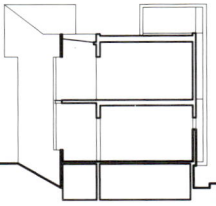

East facing courtyard

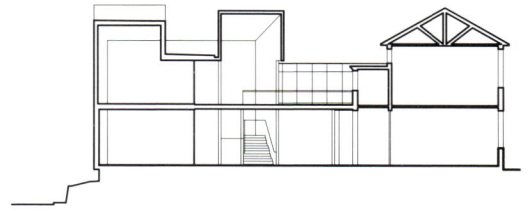

Circulation stair

Connection to existing building

Interior of Food Technology

MOTORWAY ONRAMP.   PROPOSED TECHNOLOGY.   COURTYARD.   EXISTING BLDG.

SECTION LOOKING NORTH·WEST.

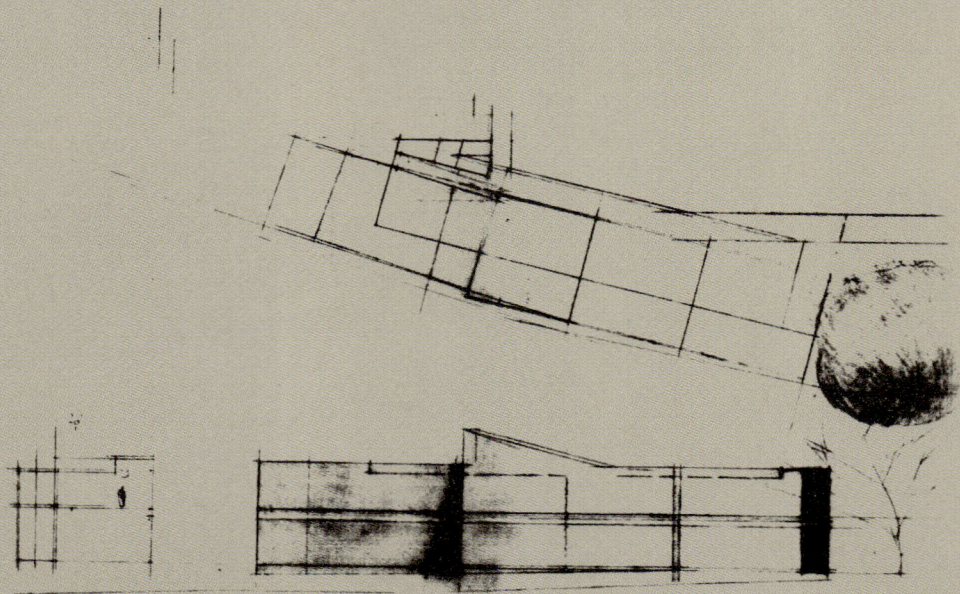

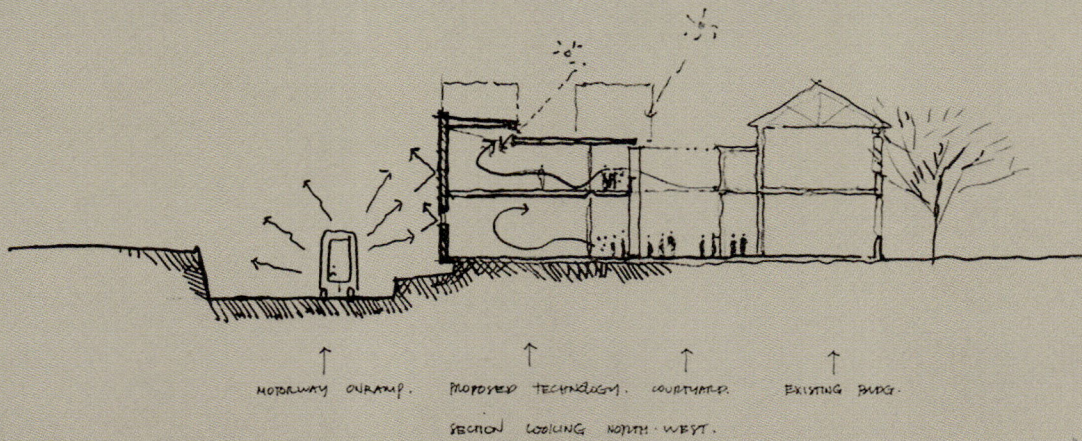

Concept sketches

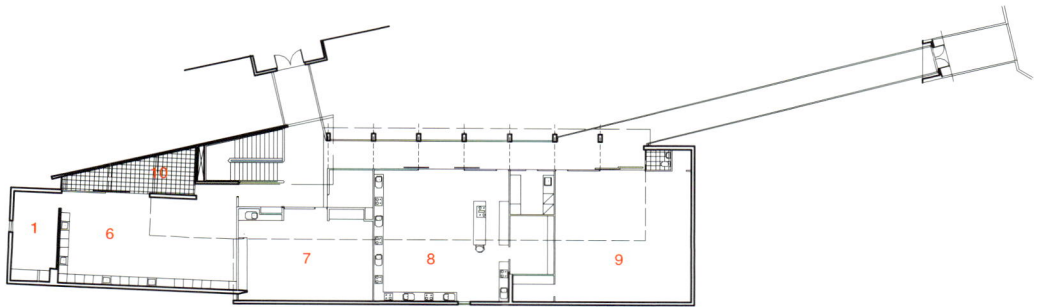

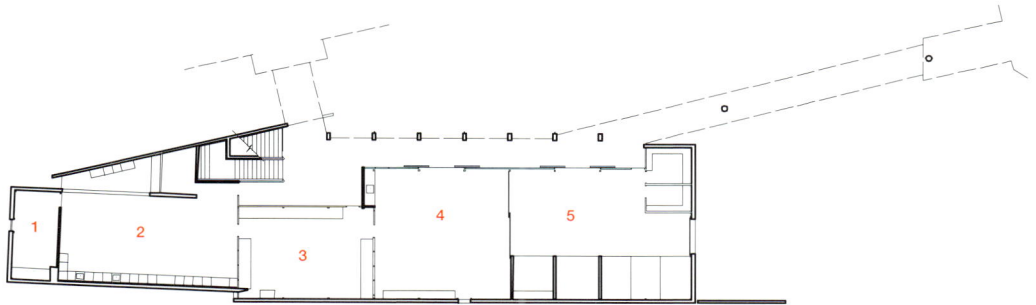

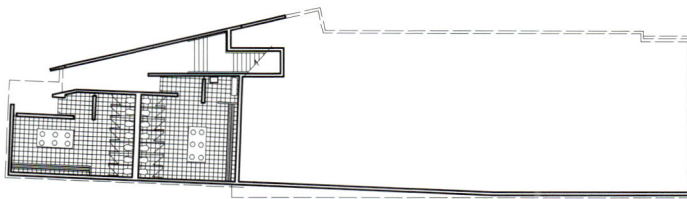

Floor plans:
Level 2
Level 1
Basement

1. Store
2. Clean materials
3. Planning and design
4. Materials general
5. Machine shop
6. Biotechnology
7. Teacher resource
8. Food technology
9. IT
10. Conservatory

View from the north-west

Middle School

THE BROTHER V.A. SULLIVAN BUILDING
ST PETER'S COLLEGE
AUCKLAND
2001 – 2003

The infrastructural and urban design issues confronting Auckland – an 'accidental city' if ever there was one – can be daunting. However, they seem less intractable when broken down into comprehensible portions. Many parts of the city's fabric work well enough as discrete elements, and they are capable of integration into larger urban segments. Patrick Clifford has described this civic amelioration from below as "a knitting together of neighbourhoods". Perhaps the best examples of Architectus' 'join the dots' approach are the buildings the practice has designed on Mountain Road for near-neighbours St Peter's College and Auckland Grammar.

Huddled into its tight site, St Peter's has not, in the past, given much of itself away. This introversion was disrupted by Architectus' Technology Block, which took the school to the very edge of the Southern Motorway. The new Middle School, which anchors the campus at its southeast corner, now gives St Peter's a defining presence on its border with Mountain Road. The L-shaped building faces into the school and towards the afternoon sun, its structure revealed but its classrooms sheltered. Along Mountain Road the façade is sterner and more formal; the leg-up offered by the high ground gave the architects the opportunity to design an 'acropolis', with thin concrete fins for columns.

With its fins and basalt-finished panels, the Middle School appears to be a resilient as well as a graceful structure (in its buildings no less than its rugby teams, St Peter's favours a muscular Christianity). The Middle School is a forceful addition to the Mountain Road streetscape, but it is assertive, not bullying. It lays strong visual claim to the rugby pitch over the road. Looming above the goal posts, it makes the ground seem more like an arena, and less like a paddock. A ground-level walkway through the building frames views of the playing field from within the campus, the visual connection compensating for physical detachment.

St Peter's Middle School gives Mountain Road impetus as it heads uphill and upmarket to Auckland Grammar. There Architectus, in a fortunate coincidence, have designed a Technology Block that addresses the street in an appropriate manner (scoria is the local construction dialect) but in a more restrained fashion ("St Peter's needed a stronger hand," Clifford says.)

This building, too, is a defining work, careful to acknowledge context but firm in establishing boundaries. Like the St Peter's Middle School, Grammar's Technology Block is strong in itself; together, the buildings make an already substantial street even more coherent.

*Adapted from an article by **John Walsh** in Architecture New Zealand, July/August 2003*

Fins and sunshades
on the west façade

View from the east

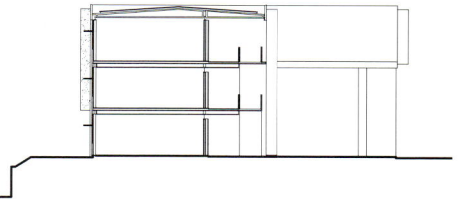

Concrete fins act as
sunshading devices
throughout the building

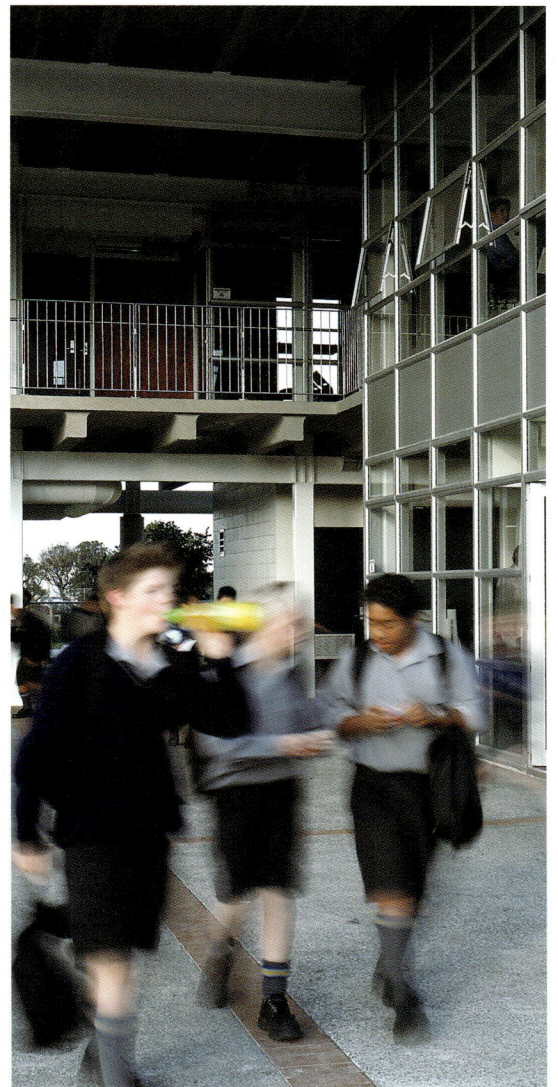

West elevation overlooks the
internal playing field

Courtyard

Concept sketches –
section and perpective

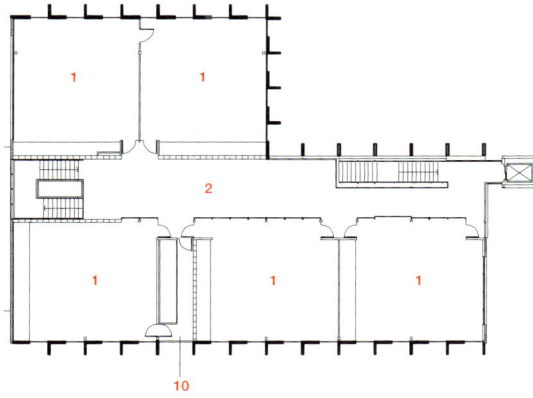

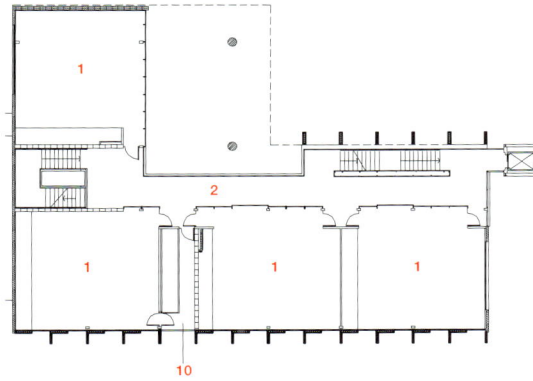

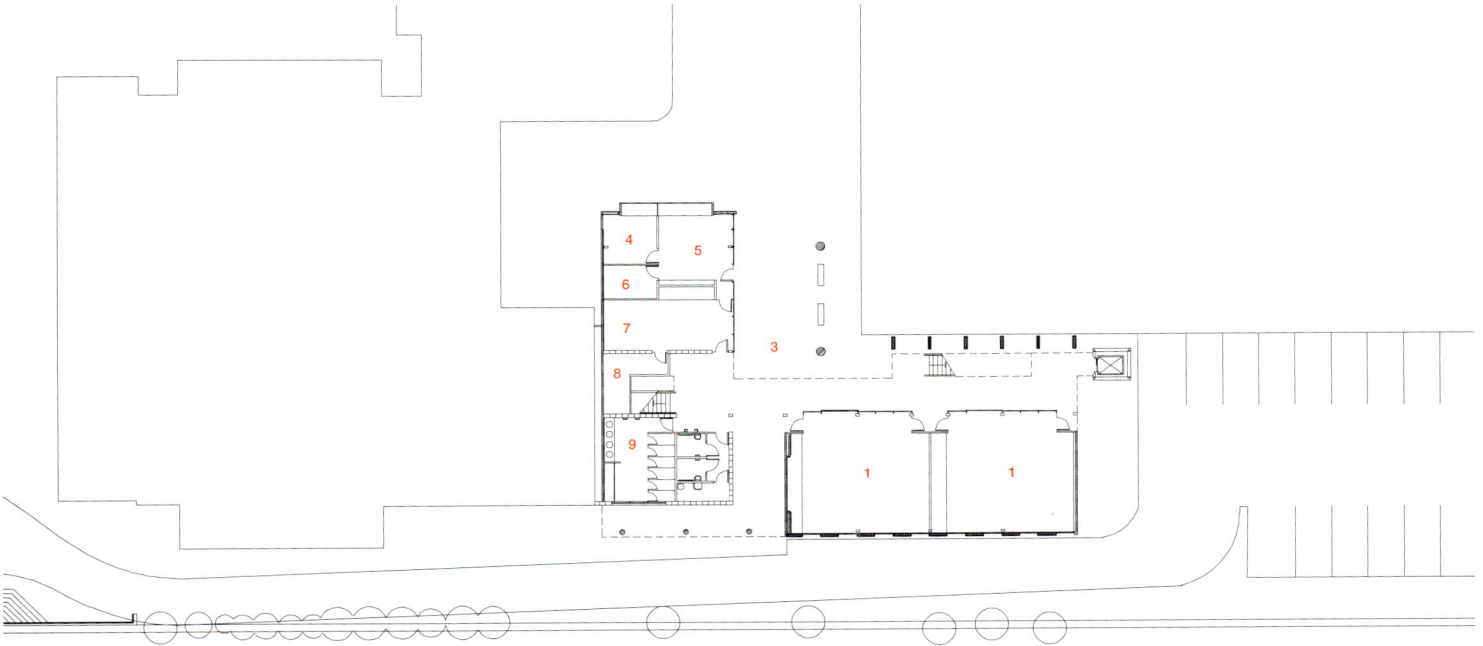

Floor plans

Level 3
Level 2
Level 1

1. Classroom
2. Walkway
3. Courtyard
4. Office
5. Reception
6. Meeting
7. Resources
8. Store
9. Toilets
10. Plant

View from north-east

New Lynn Community Centre

AUCKLAND
1999 – 2001

In a way, the architect's work on the New Lynn Community Centre comes over as a kind of civic psychoanalysis, initiating enough meaningful conversations with the client and the site in order to reveal layers of history, culture and conflict, and to initiate a process that will continue to evolve in the performance of the building. The result of this process is not only a building design, but also an exhaustive knowledge of the site and context of the project: the urban condition.

The brief from Waitakere City Council emphasised its commitment to eco-design principles and issues of sustainability of land use, specification of building materials, environment and servicing strategies, maintenance costs and the well-being of users. In this regard the New Lynn Community Centre is very much part of Architectus' recherché architecturale. The basic parti has by now informed an impressively diverse range of residential, commercial and institutional works at different scales and locations.

Despite this (or perhaps as a result of it?), each develops a clear design trategy that informs and articulates a particular programme and identity – not repetitious, but surely evolved rather than invented. The laconic formal vocabulary recalls the programmatic essentialism of Kahn or Foster, but is knowingly inflected to the troublesome realities of the local environment. At New Lynn, the building - a unified 'community of rooms' plus a vestigial porch, deck and verandah – has been generated as much by an essentially humanist attitude towards civic place and occupation as it has by site conditions, planning, sustainability, materials and local technique.

At first sight, the scale, rigour and sparseness of the building seems both indigenous and alien to its site. There remains the dry New Zealand concern for the everyday, the self-conscious local referents, but there is also lyricism, romance and an urbane, sophisticated awareness of a universal discipline of architecture. While, to others, the triangular corner site might have implied a triangular corner building, Architectus' analysis quickly suggested a layered linear arrangement running north-east to south-west, parallel to the railway line.

The existing totara reserve on the east corner was retained and re-contoured as an open amphitheatre. The main spaces – a double-height multi-purpose performance hall and a similar-scaled half-court games space – are separated from the railway by a buffer zone – an implied poche – of servant rooms, arranged enfilade and backed by an earth berm to achieve the optimum conditions for sound and vibration reduction from the railway.

Perhaps the real strength of this particular building lies in its eschewing of the more obvious features of either domestic or commercial vernacular in favour of a more, dare we say, classical vocabulary. But this is no dry formalism: it is rather evidence of a mature architectural sensibility that has evolved through the tectonic expressivity of earlier work and now seeks to imbue the character of the civil with an equally transcendental character.

Charles Walker *Architecture New Zealand, September/October 2001*

Entry courtyard and colonnade

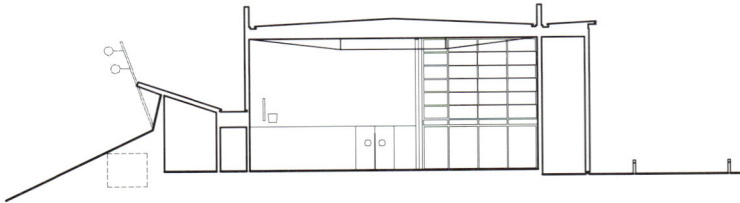

Recreation space

View from the east, the railway lines
lie to the left of the berm

Entry plaza

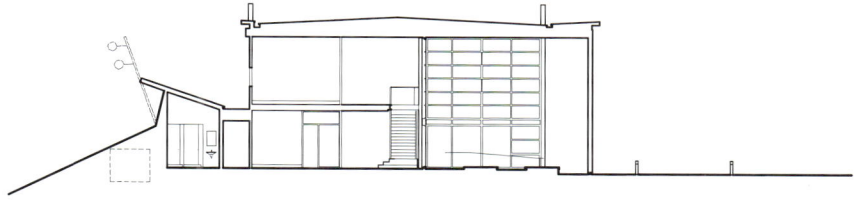

Entry courtyard

COVERED ENTRY PORCH.
FACILITY FOR PHOTO-VOLTAIC'S

HIGHLY INSULATED FABRIC

VENTILATION PATH UNDER
FLOOR TO HIGH LEVEL.

SUNSCREEN.

MEETING ROOMS ON FIRST
FLOOR.

INSULATION + SOUND DEFLECTION
VIA BERM.
POSSIBLE WATER STORAGE.

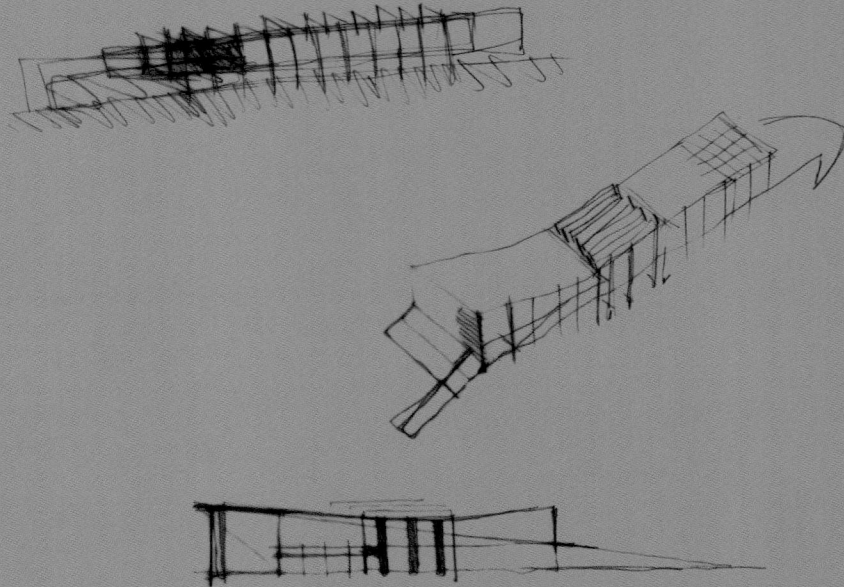

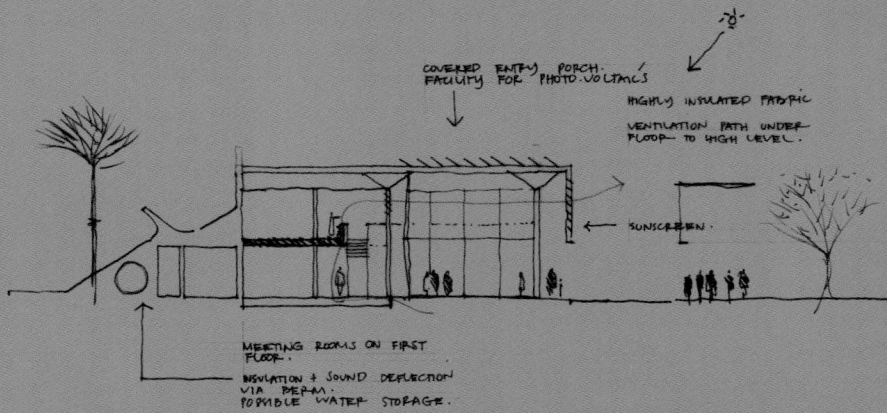

Concept sketches

Sketch of section
through entry

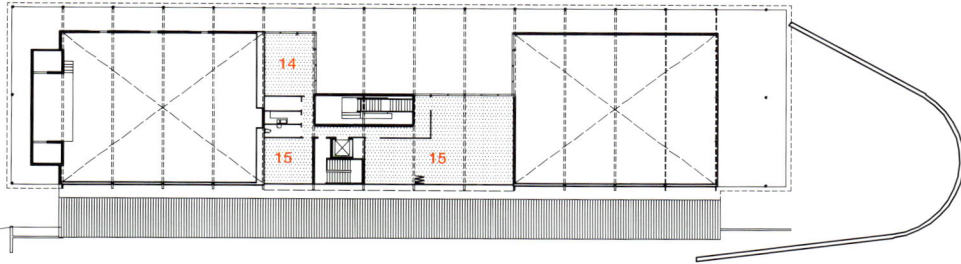

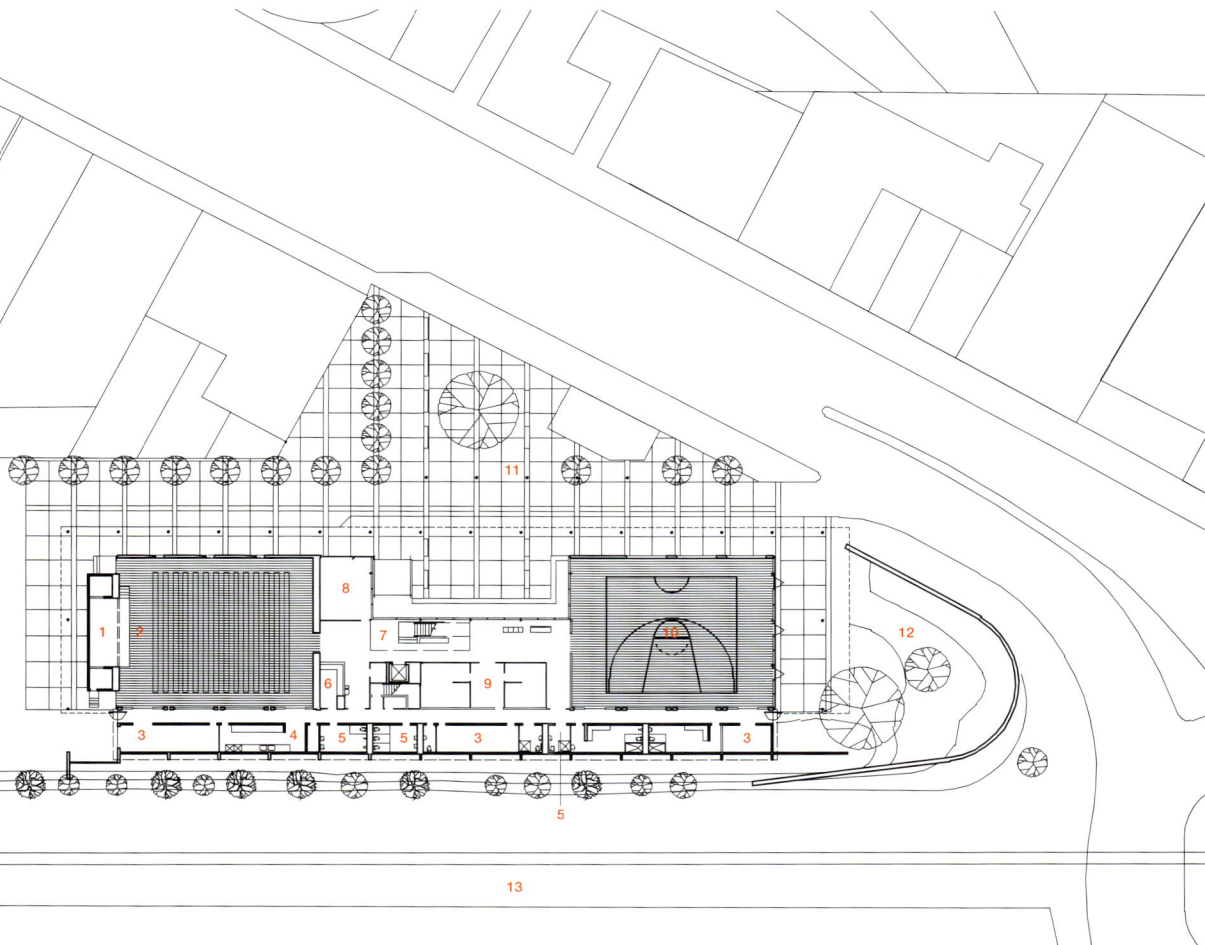

Floor plans:

Level 2

Level 1

1. Stage
2. Main hall
3. Storage/plant
4. Catering kitchen
5. Toilets/changing
6. Servery
7. Foyer
8. Office
9. Plunket
10. Active recreation space
11. New public plaza
12. Totara reserve
13. Railway line
14. Learning centre
15. Meeting rooms

View from west

Stanley Point House

AUCKLAND
1997 – 2003

"We want to build a home for our family where we feel comfortable spending most of our time. The building reflects the patterns and events of our lives and links to the environment we live in.

We envisage an honest house that shows what it is made of. Lines and spaces are beautifully proportioned and functional; clean and unadorned, yet refined; warm in their simplicity. There is a certain reductionism in the look and economy of materials and shapes.

We would like to use quality, readily available materials combined with workmanship that pays attention to detail without being 'precious'."

(From the client's brief)

Over a five-year period Architectus has, along with the client, colleagues and contractors, at times quietly, at times feverishly, worked to realise this dwelling.

The land, which abuts a reserve on one side and an unoccupied site on the other, falls from the end of a quiet no-exit street down to a smallish sea cliff and into the sea. The house inevitably does the same, while endeavouring to enrich the journey by providing places to stop along the way and offering different pathways both inside and out to choose from. In this sense of movement and journeying, the house is both object and landscape – as something to be both in and on. This is a deliberate blurring of the relationship between 'earthwork' and 'skyworks' and is reflected in the intersection and overlapping of construction and materials – blockwork and timber.

While offering choice and range, the underlying structure and organisation is simple and direct. A two-bay wide structure on four levels is stretched along the site, the degree of enclosure varied to provide a courtyard and terraces 'within' the overall form.

The inevitability of the movement of both body and eye to water, and the distance beyond, is resisted by the courtyard in particular. The living spaces are organised around this covered outdoor room providing protection from harsh light and cool breezes, while allowing the view to be enjoyed through the living space.

Walls in the long direction are generally solid, and project beyond the laminated beam structure to contain cabinetry, protect openings and allow slotted and incised views that contrast with those offered by the simply glazed crosswalls.

The roof is a plane of gravel populated by timber-clad roof lights that both emit and admit light, a reciprocity that is at the core of this project.

View from east

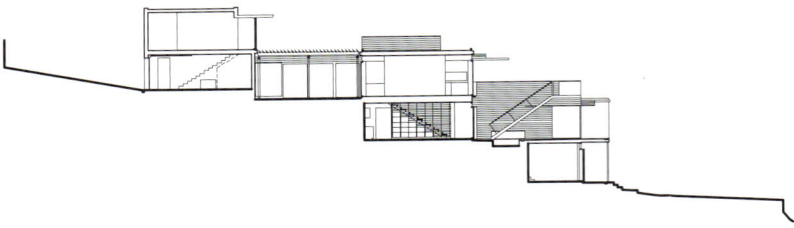

View from north

View from the north-east

Family area

Kitchen

View from west looking out across the bay

Kitchen looking south

View of courtyard from the east

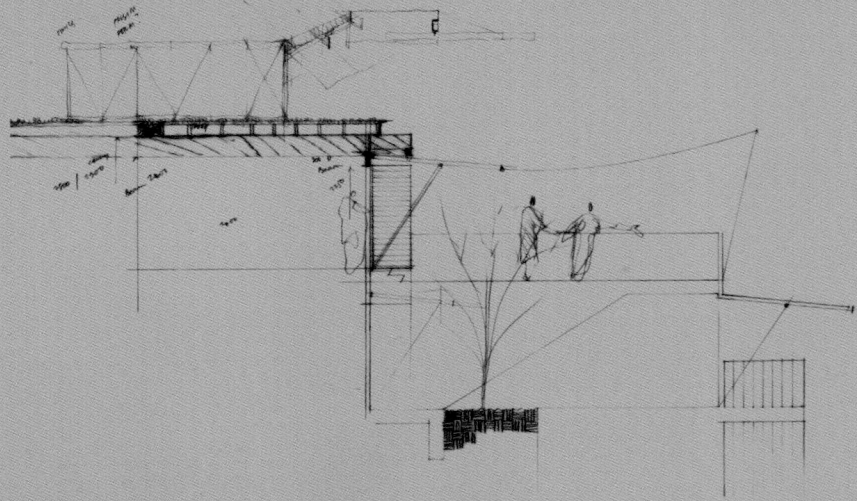

Concept sketches

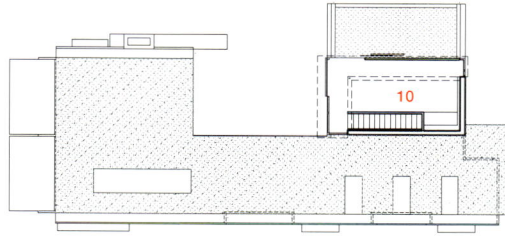

Floor plans:

Level 4

Level 3

Level 2

Level 1

1. Guest room
2. Bathroom
3. Store
4. Bedroom
5. Laundry
6. Living room
7. Kitchen/dining
8. Family

9. Garage
10. Study
11. Terrace
12. Deck
13. Pond
14. Courtyard
15. Motor court
16. Entry

Materials and Composites Research Hall

Engineering and Science Research Centre

THE UNIVERSITY OF AUCKLAND TAMAKI CAMPUS
2001 – 2003

The Engineering and Science Research Centre was the initial project carried out under the 1999 masterplan for the development of the University of Auckland's Tamaki campus. It is the first of an intended trio of economical and flexible structures capable of being put to various uses – training, research, academic/business partnerships – in different spatial configurations. Together, the three buildings will constitute a 'mini-campus' on the south-east edge of the Tamaki site, adjacent to a light-industrial district and next to a designated motorway corridor.

The 3000m² (100 metres x 30 metres) building presents an aggregate-finished pre-cast concrete face to the site's tough eastern boundary. Along the west side, facing into the campus, a wall of glass opens to a colonnade running the length of the building. The roof's curved bowspring trusses allow light to be brought into the building; the long, repetitive sweep of wave-like shapes distinguish the Research Centre from adjacent industrial boxes.

The building's modular design will accommodate changes of use, and of individual users' requirements, over time.

(Design for the Engineering and Science Research Centre was completed and construction was under way before the tenants were determined.) It comprises 10 bays; the primary bays are spaces measuring 20 metres x 10 metres, with a clear height of 7.2 metres. These primary bays provide the main space for each module. Directly accessible from a loop road and able to accommodate heavy machinery, the bays can operate as discrete units or be combined with any of the secondary bay options. The secondary bays, 10 metres x 10 metres x 7.2 metres high, may be divided into two floors to incorporate teaching spaces and offices, or may be opened into primary bays, providing additional high clearance workshop space with a smaller mezzanine area.

The building incorporates environmentally sustainable and energy efficient principles. Wherever possible, materials derived from sustainable resources, or materials that are easily recyclable, were specified. Natural ventilation, sun shades and thermal insulation were employed. Light, airy, and flexible, the building and its planned siblings immediately earned the (affectionate) title of 'The Barns'.

Aerial view of site showing the PHC building (top) and the Engineering & Science Research Centre

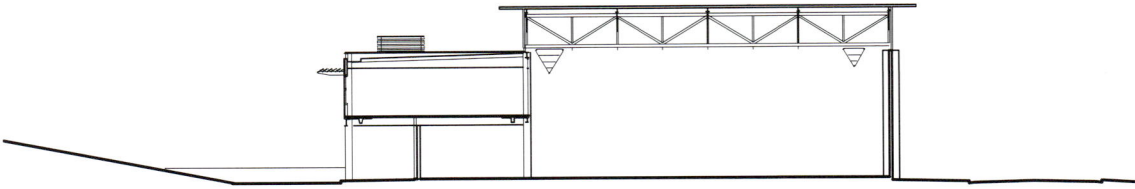

View from west

View from east

View from the north-west

INITIAL CONSTRUCTION 20M X 50M = 1000M²

GLAZED WALL

DEVELOPMENT OF
ANCILLARY + SERVICE ZONE

CURVED TRUSSES
SPAN ONTO 20M
TUBULAR TRUSS

INTERMEDIATE FLOORS
CAN BE ADDED.

0 2 4 6 8 10M.

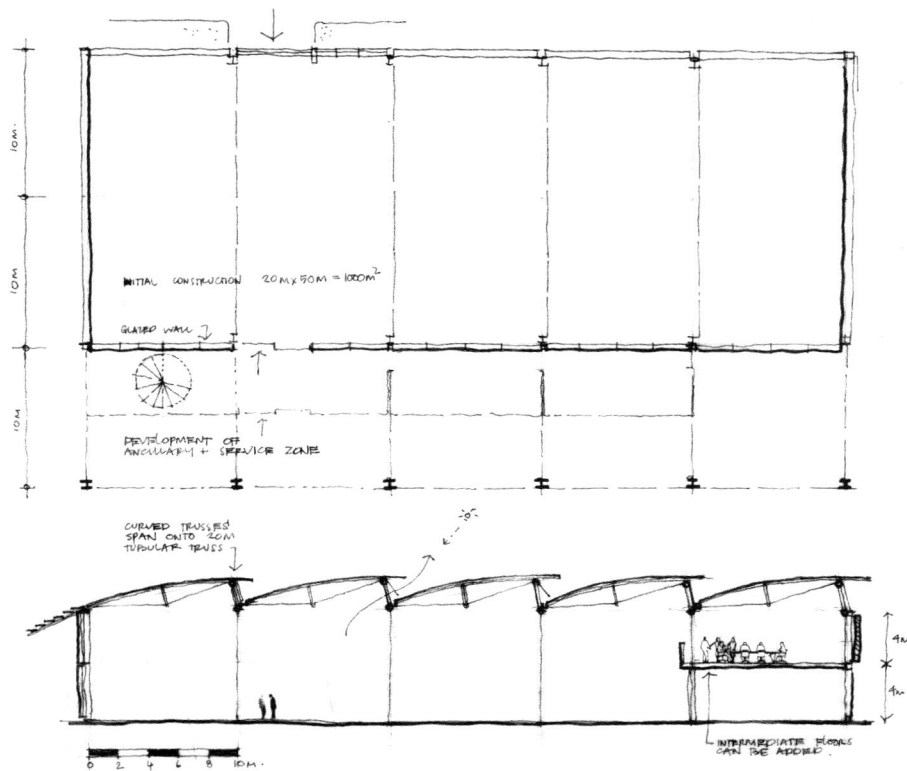

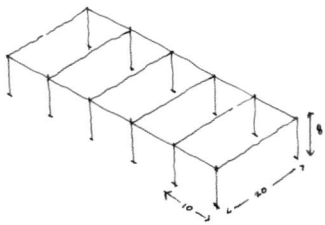

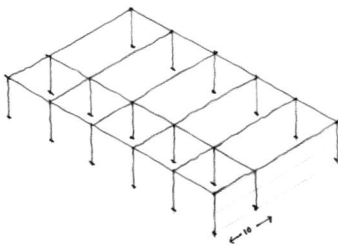

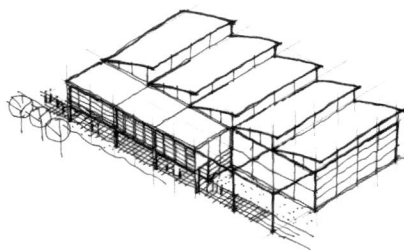

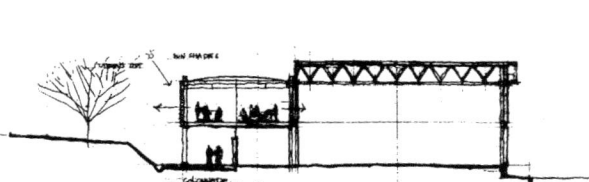

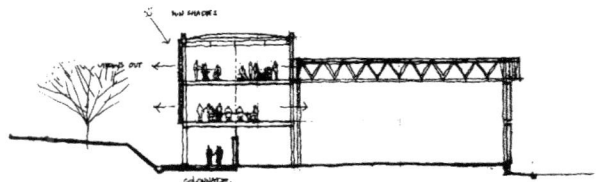

Early conceptual plan and
section showing five bays

Primary bay and secondary bay options

Possible three-level secondary bay

Model viewed from the north

Population Health Complex

THE UNIVERSITY OF AUCKLAND TAMAKI CAMPUS
2002 – DUE FOR COMPLETION 2004 (UNDER CONSTRUCTION)

The Population Health Complex (PHC), a post-graduate research and training facility with 300 work and 500 seminar spaces, occupies and signifies a prominent location on the University of Auckland's Tamaki campus. The 10,000m² building, the second project carried out under the campus master-plan, provides a 'gateway' to a site that has been rather amorphous. It is a pivotal structure, designed to be expressive of itself, but also to accommodate existing neighbours on one side and anticipate future buildings on the other.

The building traverses its corner site in a boomerang-shaped curve; the analogy, developed with Rewi Thompson, is that of a wrap-around cloak. (The campus borders suburbs that historically have had a high proportion of Maori and Pacific Island residents.) In a gesture to existing buildings, this public elevation is bookended with concrete panels finished in white aggregate. Sections of brick cladding also offer some material continuity. Vertical concrete 'fins' provide articulation to the facade and rhythm to its progress; they also have a functional purpose as lower-level sunshades.

The heart of the complex is the triangular central atrium which links all levels, bringing light and air into the complex. Materials are simple and robust: concrete and glass; stone tiles for the atrium floor;

wooden louvres on internal windows; plywood panels, in a subtle basketweave pattern, on the atrium's internal façade. The atrium responds to the client's desire for an 'open building', which encourages communication and cooperation among staff and students, and which is welcoming to users of the PHC's public clinics.

The PHC will be, demonstrably, a busy building, and also a flexible one, combining private ('cellular') and open-plan ('clustered') work spaces, and seminar and study areas. It is also designed to be a healthy building. Passive environmental controls include sunshades, awnings and openable windows, while hollow concrete floor beams provide high thermal mass to mediate temperature fluctuations and double as ductwork for the delivery of tempered fresh air.

Two wings reach out from the atrium into the interior of the site, and towards the series of existing H-shaped buildings. The wings frame an internal courtyard, which provides another sociable space for the PHC's inhabitants and visitors. In their height and rectilinear nature, these wings or 'fingers' are compatible with the existing buildings. Connecting with the axes of those buildings, the new wings define the spine running through the north side of the campus and bring it into the sheltering curve of the 'cloak'.

View from the north

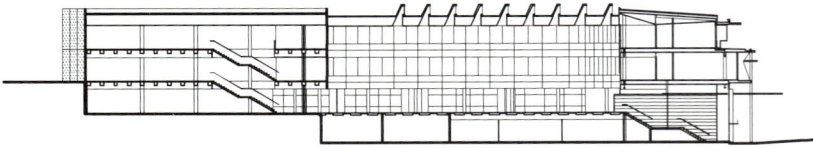

Main atrium

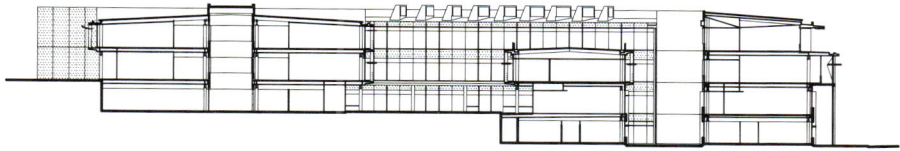

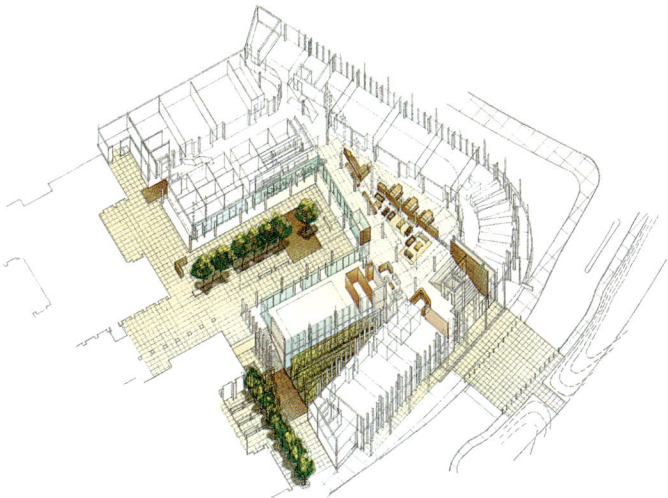

Landscape axonometric

Small courtyard

View from east | Atrium skylights

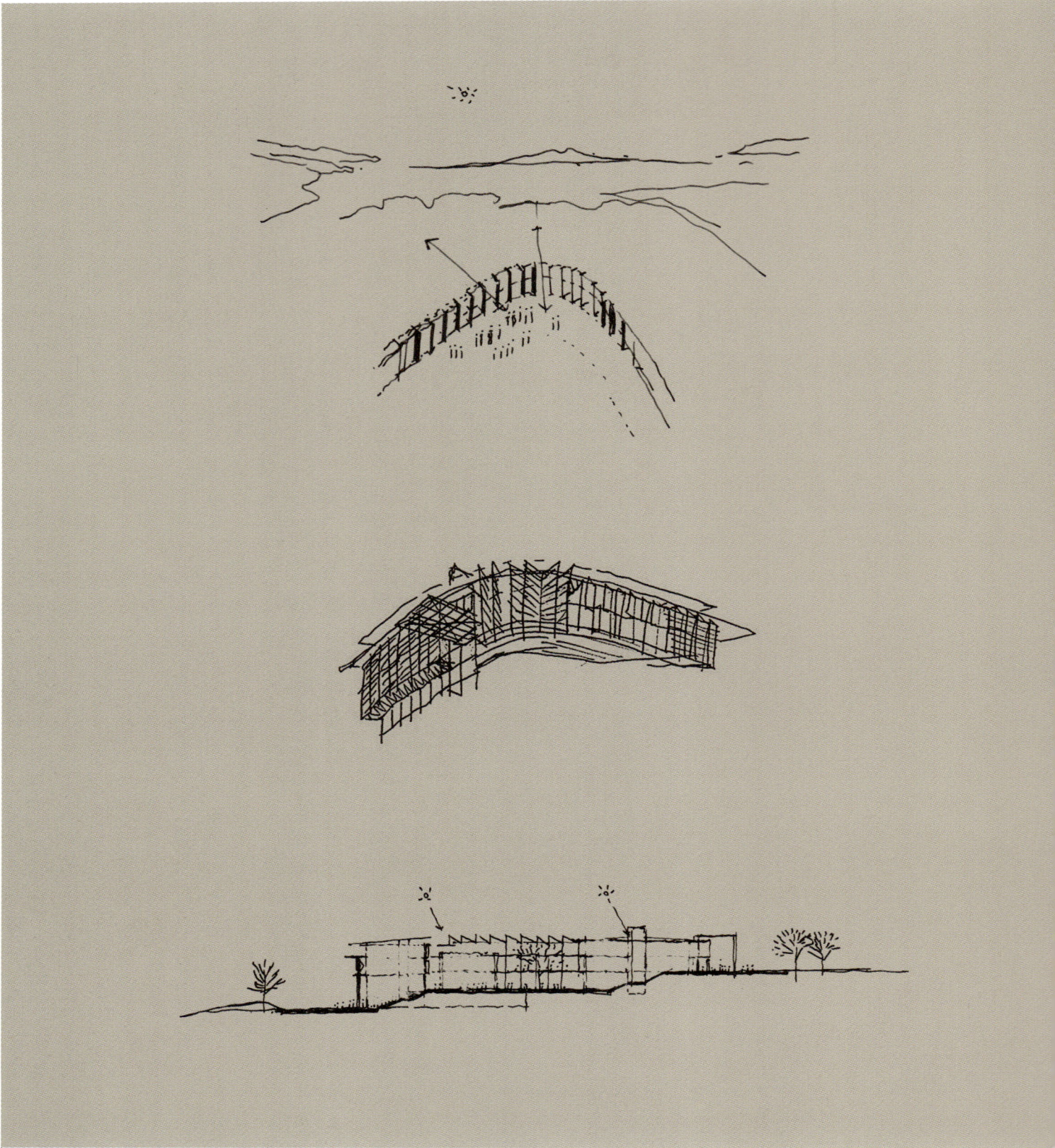

Conceptual sketches and section

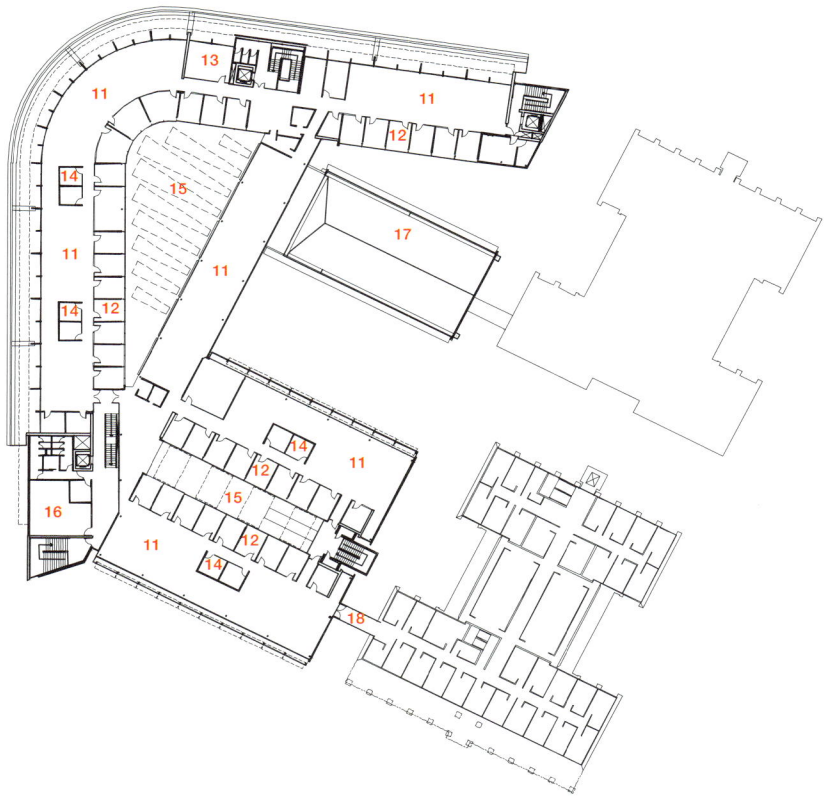

Floor plans:

Level 4

Level 2

1. Entry
2. Atrium
3. Courtyard
4. Reception
5. Seminar room
6. Lecture/function room
7. Study area and journal display
8. Computer room
9. Break-out room
10. Café and seating
11. Clustered workspaces
12. Cellular office
13. Meeting
14. Interview room
15. Void with skylights
16. Plant
17. Roof
18. Link to existing buildings
19. Campus spine

Design

Architect David Mitchell
discussion with Patrick Clifford

"I certainly did not
have the knowledge
to even realise it
was possible to
study architecture,
to practise at it and
become better."

David Mitchell: *Some architects look to their clients for sources of architectural ideas, some look into their memories, some at buildings and building types in history. Some turn literary ideas into architectural metaphors or representations, and I suppose some just try to pluck something from thin air. What do you do?*

Patrick Clifford: Inevitably a combination of some of those things you note. I think it is true in our case that the opportunity and ability to use architectural references has developed as our knowledge and experience has increased.

My recollection of architecture school would be that while the culture did not encourage an 'in the mode of' approach, or support it with history and a strong engagement with our own context, I certainly did not have the knowledge to even realise it was possible to study architecture, to practise at it and become better, as it were. Without that knowledge and in an environment where design was presented as a personal expression, we relied on analogy and image primarily.

Other sources of ideas are myths and legends, cultural practice, interest in ways of building, structure and environment, and hopefully an increasing ability to understand and recognise the opportunities of context. The exploration of space is able to be thought about in the context of a body of architectural knowledge and the context of passion for that knowledge. In respect to sources generally, as Michael Sorkin used to say, "It's not what you do that counts, it's how you do it." The source itself is simply that – a place to begin from or a connection that can be translated into architecture.

The work at Canterbury University illustrates a couple of approaches: the Mathematics Building developed from finding the particulars of the way the users wanted to work and teach, and developing a model for that. This 'close' reading of the brief and looking for pieces we can emphasise or give importance to is one way we work.

The adjacent Sciences Library is built around the idea of a bookcase – albeit a large, over-scaled one. It recalls and preserves the notion of the library as a repository or storehouse in the age of the information commons; a metaphorical anchoring around which other concerns evolve.

The idea of earth work and sky work is a powerful influence. Renzo Piano talks of this and there are so many examples – the Sydney Opera House, and other Jorn Utzon projects of course.

In our own case, I think the Museum in Wellington and the recreation centre at UNITEC (both competitions) work with that idea. Our own house also, preparing the ground and then building on it.

I liked Charles Walker's report on your New Lynn Community Centre. The client commented on seeing the initial design drawings that they lacked the 'wow' factor. "The architects patiently explain that they don't do wow." You didn't even do 'wow' as a student. You were more of a slow burner holding the heat than a box of fireworks waiting to be lit. Quite a few dropped the match in the cracker

UNITEC Recreation Centre

box of course, but I digress. Isn't the world of 'wow' the architectural stratos-phere, the pinnacle of hope, daring and pleasure? What other position can you take? Is it enough to look at architecture as a craft? What goals do you hold dear as you bend over the board?

That comment regarding the 'wow' factor will of course haunt us. The kind of 'wow' we were dealing with was at the level of the curved roof or the angled wall. The Christchurch Art Gallery is an example of the 'wow' factor. The curved roof and angled wall have been used brilliantly – our comment relates to the perception that architecture without these devices cannot possibly be 'wow'.

When I look at the work of someone like Peter Zumthor I think 'wow', yet I do not think the drawings of his art museum in Bregenz would have cut much ice with too many New Zealand local authorities.

Having said that, we did get to build the Community Centre and the odd person has said they like it – I could not swear that was a 'wow' exclamation.

I do not know what the pinnacle of hope, daring and pleasure is, but I do know we have taken and continue to take risks that we hope will bring pleasure, at least. Of course, by now we know how close failure is and that in architecture, at least, risk does not necessarily bring rewards.

Architecture as craft is not enough but we believe that the practice of archi-tecture is craft and we hold that dear.

What else? The challenge? The excitement of opening that brief document and contemplating, finding, cajoling, or stumbling on to a way of making something out of it. We hold dear, even if it might seem few others do, that what we are doing is important, that it is long lasting and demands care accordingly. We hold dear what we have done, with some exceptions, and the collective experience of that.

I recall once saying to you that I found a lot of Australian houses summary in their planning, by which I meant thin and diagrammatic. "But that's the aim," you said. I took it you were applauding succinctness, since I knew you wouldn't want thinness.

I remembered that conversation while looking at recent Architectus plans. They are often very clearly organised – summary in the flattering sense. Systematic constructional methods, and formal austerity, with a restricted palette seems characteristic of the buildings, and I see a clear line of descent from mainline Modernism of the not-yet-popular 1960s. There are the 'served' and 'service' spaces of Kahn, the sparseness of the Smithsons at Hunstanton, the New Brutalist concrete work of Sir Miles Warren, and perhaps even a stress on the plan as generator that was once common.

I am inclined to see this as a position, both in favour of certain things and against others. (Frank Gehry and Howard Raggatt seem a long way off). How do Archi-tectus see it?

New Lynn Community Centre

House on Waiheke Island

Perhaps when we had that conversation I was recalling your reference to the plan of the Rotherham House as being "summary" – which I, possibly incorrectly, took to be the thin reference rather than the succinct one.

Having only relatively recently become familiar with that house, I thought that the plan was dense and powerful – achieving so much with very modest means. Perhaps I also felt it easy to gloss over the ease with which that appeared to be done and overlook its intensity and refinement.

We probably, purposefully, use the term plan, and think about the plan in a way that others refer to parti – the diagram is drawn like a plan but refers to, and implies, volume and form, space and structure. If there is to be a summary description of our intention it is to build density. At a kind of practical level we have found the strong plan/parti to be a liberating thing. Like all architects we deal with the demands of clients, demands that change for many reasons. We try to give ourselves a framework that is conceptually and intellectually able to withstand interrogation, and survive.

The idea of being 'against' things does not feature in our thoughts. Of course it can be convenient to take solace in dismissing other approaches after losing a competition or having some other kind of bad day. That is not to say we are ambivalent about what we do and how, nor that Frank Gehry and Howard Raggatt can seem a long way off – they seem to me to be just as far from each other as they are from us though.

Your take-off of some of our influences is accurate and there are others. We are inspired and challenged by Bilbao and Canberra. Are we wasting time in our little world, should we get Ciata (the modelling programme they use – or religion in Howard's case) and get on with it? We have seen enough mighty struggles with the narrative and sculptural models to know it's not that easy. This is not to say that the architecture you mention is not an influence either – we have been quite clear about references and sources. The principle of acknowledgement is important to us.

To go back to the first question, Gehry makes very clear plans.

You may have been disadvantaged by an education that fostered 'self expression', but people tend to get more interested in history as they get older. Can you identify some of the world architectural history that now interests you, and tell me how it shows in Architectus buildings?

I did not mean to complain of an education that fostered self-expression. We are not trying to claim disadvantaged status even if we might need it.

Influences fall into two categories: fundamental founding forces, and those we dip into or temporarily fall for. What is interesting is the dynamic nature of the interaction with history. We are always expanding our knowledge back in time and with time.

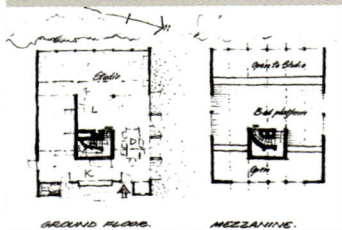

"If there is to be a summary description of our intention, it is to build density."

Rotherham House, *Bruce Rotherham*

Last year I was able to visit Finland and Alvar Aalto's work for the first time, which of course led me to study it. On the same trip I saw work by Steven Holl, Renzo Piano, Herzog & de Meuron and Norman Foster. Earlier this year Denys Lasdun caught my attention.

I had the opportunity to visit some of the California Modernists – Schindler, Ellwood and others, but most memorably, the Salk Institute by Louis Kahn. Just down the road, almost as an aside (and I do not imply any disrespect), was Williams and Tsien's Neurosciences Building.

I'd like to know what qualities, and movements, and particular buildings in New Zealand architecture have influenced you too? Do you see yourself as a part of an architectural tradition?

To answer the last part first, we most definitely see ourselves as part of a tradition and we are happy to be quite conscious in developing our relationship with that tradition. This occurs not only through knowledge of historical examples and contemporary practice but also through numerous collaborations with colleagues that have both enriched and instructed our work. Without sounding too self important, we also feel responsible for helping develop that tradition. Qualities we refer to include the lightness and sparseness of the regional modern houses of the Fifties, while at the same time being committed to the weight and expressiveness of Christchurch and Dunedin in the Sixties.

We feel less influenced by the work of the Seventies and Eighties, yet it had more of an affect on our own education and training than any other period – particularly through Marshall Cook and Terry Hitchcock, from whom we gained the opportunity to begin and an appreciation of the past. Marshall Cook's own house is not so much an influence as a benchmark. Numerous Warren and Mahoney buildings such as the Crematorium, Christchurch College, the Student Union at Auckland University, and indeed, given our desire to practise in the public realm, the universities, particularly Auckland, Canterbury and Dunedin, have been specially influential – not just for the individual work but equally for the places that are made by these collections. As our work progresses, our interest is increasingly turning to that which lies beyond the site.

From a personal viewpoint there were many hours of my youth spent carefully observing churches such as F. de J. Clere's St Mary of the Angels and John Scott's Futuna Chapel in Wellington. More recently the Catholic Cathedral in Christchurch gave Jade Stadium some of its scale, while the work around the Government Centre in Wellington, particularly low-rise office buildings like Duncan Joiner's William Clayton Building, affected my thinking about the work at Canterbury. Increasingly we believe it will be the work of our peers that will inform our work.

David Mitchell is an Auckland architect who has designed a number of well-known buildings. He wrote 'The Elegant Shed' (on New Zealand architecture from 1945-84), and presented a television series of the same name. He taught architecture at Auckland University from 1972-87, and was an adjunct professor at UNITEC School of Architecture in 2001 and 2002.

"…we most definitely see ourselves as part of a tradition and we are happy to be quite conscious in developing our relationship with that tradition."

Christchurch College,
Warren and Mahoney Architects

Drawing

Amanda Hyde de Kretser
discussion with Patrick Clifford

"I think we saw
the work and
the drawings
as being quite
connected."

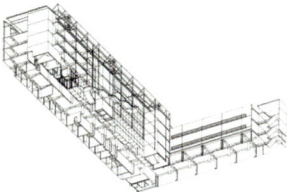

Amanda Hyde de Kretser: *Patrick, drawing and modelling have obviously had significant roles in the development of the architecture that Architectus is producing today. I am interested in exploring the character of these roles a little further. Can I take you back to your undergraduate thesis? I understand that it was in the field of drawing.*

Patrick Clifford: Yes, we were at architecture school Post Modernism was on everybody's minds. There was a lot of talk about drawings and presentation of architectural projects in drawing form. This coincided with the feeling I had at university that drawing was treated with a degree of suspicion. There was almost a sense that if the drawing was good then perhaps the project wasn't.

So your thesis was questioning that?

Not so much questioning but rather exploring these issues. I can draw, so I thought that I wouldn't mind having a look at the role of drawing in architecture. I didn't think drawings were covering anything up – you can take a very ordinary project and draw it well but it's still a very ordinary project.

In student work I find that a well-drawn project usually equates to a well-understood project. There seems to be a relationship between drawing and understanding. You have spoken also about a very strong and necessary relationship between travelling and drawing that touches on understanding. What are you really getting at here?

Well, I think it was quite a literal thing. I had observed that drawing and travel was something that architects have done through history. They travel and they draw. I must say at the outset I didn't really know quite why. I have, of course, discovered it is common knowledge among those who draw and travel that the process of drawing enables understanding and creates memories.

You speak very freely about the use of precedents in the development of the architecture of Architectus. It is interesting to see that you similarly use the drawing styles of the architects you have learnt from. When you were developing a project 'in the manner of' Charles Moore we see that your drawings were similarly 'in the manner of' Charles Moore. I'm interested to discover whether you found that, by drawing like these architects, you understood more about their architecture? Do you believe that the association between the drawing style and the architecture was a necessary association?

We saw the work and the drawing as being quite connected. So, if you are interested in Charles Moore and you get the book *The Place of Houses*, you learn about and look at the projects through the axonometric drawing. So, it seems pretty natural that you'll then draw in that way.

How far do you think you took this? I knew you were interested in Aalto's work so I looked a little closer at his drawings and I found that there were similarities between Aalto's drawings and the drawings of Architectus, even in terms of composition. Aalto's drawings and some of your drawings appear to be higher on the page than might be expected. The viewer's understanding of space can be drawn from the way the drawing is placed on the page.

I don't think we've gone that far consciously. I am always aware of where you put the drawing on the page. Commonly, elevations sit at the bottom of the page because that's where the ground is. However, Frank Lloyd Wright would have a huge amount of space under the drawing to give the impression of looking up. If you look at the Spanish architects they'll have the plan in the middle of the page and then fold out the elevations, so that you turn the page around to see them. By looking at a lot of things you absorb a lot of influences. Awareness of composition has changed now because of the computer, where you usually end up drawing and then organising the drawings at the end. When you are drawing by hand you have to figure out how the drawings relate to each other first. That was one of the real skills that architects could have – the ability to see in advance where the drawing was going to go and which bits you needed where.

The work of Louis Kahn has obviously had a strong influence on Architectus. I am wondering if you can tell me a little more about what you have described as designing through the 'extrusion of the plan'.

Perhaps describing the design process as 'an extrusion of the plan' is overly simplifying the process because it involves quite a complex set of circum-stances. When I was first exposed to this process I was working on a competition. The guy I was working with appeared to be drawing away at only one part of the plan and then suddenly there was this quite intricate conception of the entire building. What I came to realise was that the process was more of revealing the implications of the moves made in the plan. Of course you can take all sorts of plans and try to do this to them but they are not all going to produce the kinds of forms that Kahn produced. I began to realise that the plan was a kind of imprint that had the potential to have a whole lot of things embedded in it. You could produce a quite simple diagram in plan but it implied a whole range of three dimensional and formal moves.

When you speak about the early days of Architectus you make a number of references to the struggle you had as you sought a means of expression for your architecture. You seemed to be trying out a number of different architectural languages and similarly every building was drawn differently. Your early drawings seem to reflect that struggle in a way that is not evident today.

Yes, I think that now we've just stopped worrying about it. Well, perhaps not so much not worrying about it, but maybe now the issues are different. Having said that, we still talk about drawing. Shall we draw it by hand, shall we draw it on the computer, how should we… In the early days we were looking at examples and thinking…"Ah, what's this?" What we probably didn't realise is that all the buildings we were looking at had been redrawn for the books. So we would look at say a Richard Meier book – one of the things in terms of drawings that we really liked and still like from a graphical point of view – and we would think that everything looked really worked out. We now realise that the buildings had been redrawn for the book anyway.

"What I came to realise was that the process was more one of revealing the implications of the moves made in the plan."

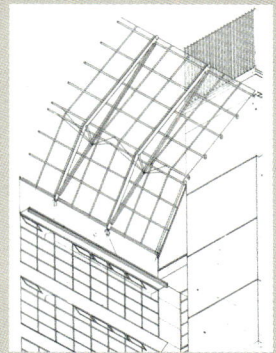

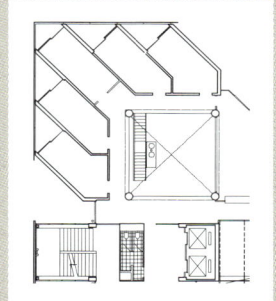

MSCS atrium

MSCS part plan

So having a forum to publish enables you to draw architecture in a way that you might not otherwise draw it?

Yes, yes...

Prior to that, you were drawing for yourself in order to understand what you were designing. You're then drawing for a client, presumably in order to communicate with them. At some point when you publish you get an opportunity to communicate in an entirely different way.

Yes, that is also the competition realm. We have thought quite a bit about presentation at this level. When you do competitions you're not present at the judging and you don't have a pre-existing relationship with the client. You just give them your project and they look at it. That means there's a requirement for the work to reach a certain level for it to be credible, and the means of presentation that can achieve this keeps changing.

When did modelling become important for Architectus? Your models suddenly start appearing in the early Nineties and appearing prolifically. Was this anything to do with you beginning to enter competitions?

Yes, they really started with the Museum of New Zealand competition in 1989. It was an incredibly complex building, which required a perspective that a model could best demonstrate. It became obvious to us that architectural models were important at a variety of levels.

Was that connected to a period when models began to be used by students at the university?

Probably. We had Mahendra Daji and James Fenton working with us at the time, who were both at university. But models in practice probably influenced models in the school as well. In general, architectural production models became quite prevalent. Architectus initially started making models of the whole building and then we got quite interested in making parts of the building as well. We have evolved a modelling approach that is to do with the materials and a certain degree of literalism. We generally do not try to build what is traditionally called presentation models. We've always tried to make models that were for our benefit. I don't quite know why or how that came about. We built three models for the Museum of New Zealand. There was a big sectional model and two other quite abstract models. In that competition we saw a number of white plastic models with model boats, model buildings and a model city. Our model was made of wire mesh and other things that we thought had some relationship to what we hoped the actual building might be made of. We have always made models in our office up until the last minute of the deadline. We have never been able to finish drawings two weeks before a competition is due and therefore be able to give them to a professional model maker.

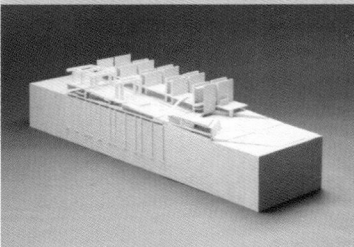

So, it seems that this process by which you make a model and the process

Victoria University Art Gallery

Te Papa Tongarewa

by which you do a drawing ends up having a strong influence on how you can design.

I don't think there is any kind of doubt about that.

I think the issue is whether or not one is conscious of the relationship between one's modelling style, or drawing style, and the architecture that one produces, or unconscious of it. I think what you are saying is that the model style you use is related to an early understanding of the building's materiality. So very early on materiality is able to become a major determinant in your architecture. This is significantly different from the white plastic model that you referred to earlier, which consciously or unconsciously suspends an exploration of materiality until a later stage in the design process. In the process of prioritising form over materiality or materiality over structure, the architect determines the way the design will develop.

Yes, I think we, at times, emphasise pieces or aspects of the project. We might make a quick model out of foam core but it is very likely that as time goes by we'll start to take some of those bits off, swap them over, add bits and modify it, so that it can do a few more things.

With students, that is not always the case. They've seen an interesting modelling technique and they use it because it looks good. They are not necessarily aware of the implications that are attached to their choices.

Right, but that's a necessary process of discovery.

For students the model develops a form of objecthood that is stronger than the architecture it refers to. Context is often excluded in response to judgements about the aesthetics of the model. The scale of the model is also understandably related to the cost of the materials. The smaller scale, however, then causes the student to see the model as an object from the outside rather than from the inside, which is perhaps more important for a form of architecture that is interested in the technology of humanism. The model of the high-rise that you did with Billy Apple and Architecture Workshop exhibits some of these qualities but in that case it reflected your desire to understand the building as a work of art. That model appears to be consciously different to most of your models in which you seem to give equal priority to the spaces beyond the programme of the specific building that you are working on.

Yes, we are doing a big competition at the moment. The base is all made and all the buildings are made around the edges. The models we are doing today are just getting bigger and bigger as we find that we need to make references to more and more of the surrounding area. Hopefully there is a limit to this!

Amanda Hyde de Kretser is a senior lecturer in visual communication and philosophy at the School of Architecture UNITEC. She has practised and taught in Los Angeles and completed a Ph.D in Architecture in 2003.

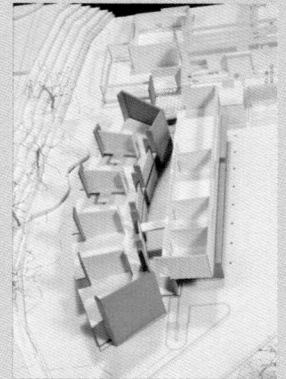

TSSC Building

High Rise Proposal, Wellington

Tectonics

Jeanette Budgett discussion with Malcolm Bowes, Patrick Clifford and Michael Thomson

"I don't think we're representing it. We're just making it. We're just doing it."

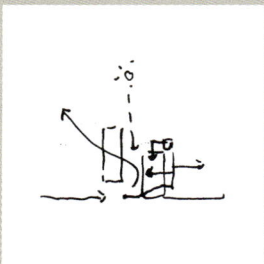

Jeanette Budgett: *The recent work of Architectus has displayed an enviable tectonic clarity, the MSCS Building and the New Lynn Community Centre to name just two projects. Your ability to crystallise a scheme into a diagram would seem to be an important starting point. Can you talk about this?*

Patrick Clifford: I think it's enjoyable and challenging, when you've got a complex brief, to turn it into something you can either draw in a couple of seconds or describe to somebody in a sentence.

Michael Thomson: You have to do that. To do a decent building you've got to distil it down to a couple of ideas.

PC: Intellectually I think it's really challenging as well. It's got to be a good diagram. For us, diagram means parti in the broadest architectural sense of intention, not the two-dimensional bubble diagram. It implies structure and many other things.

In the process of making the diagram, an apparent ordering of elements seems to occur. The New Lynn Community Centre might represent a vision for a community that is based on an orderly, civilised and transparent way of conducting ourselves. Are you interested in representing order?

PC: No, I don't think we're representing it. We're just making it. We're just doing it. Somebody else could have achieved those things – transparency, civitas, optimism – with a different, disorderly building. I don't think that's our proposition. We don't feel that it has to be like that.

There are certain strategies that you use, like symmetry and repetition, which reinforce orderliness. We see it in your own house at Kelvin Road, at New Lynn and in the towers of the MSCS Building.

PC: There's absolutely no question about it. We're interested in ordering. The bell would toll if we said we weren't, that it just happened by chance. Generally we organise all service functions together. We have discovered that the typical client/architect project relationship is dynamic and things change all the time. The organising strategy serves us very well when there is a place for it to be worked out in. We have found that this ordering doesn't take away freedom. It gives us freedom.

Your interest in dealing with service or servant space brings to mind Rem Koolhaas' comment about the suspended ceiling space of the high-rise as the zone lost to architecture. He speaks of our need to reclaim it. You do that to some extent in the MSCS Building with the pre-cast concrete ceiling panels don't you?

PC: Yes, we felt that if you handed over 30 percent of the project budget to the services engineers then it was an opportunity lost. We began saying, what if we got these services to do more than one job? If you can make the floor construction the ceiling, then there are obvious synergies. There are some relatively low impact energy strategies that can save money as well. By organising the MSCS Building so that the spaces that needed mechanical ventilation were all in the same part of the plan, we saved a lot of money. Other buildings that the University was doing had one ventilated room next to an unventilated space, which meant pipes were going everywhere. We also have a strategy for getting the orientation right, just as you would do with a house.

Your interest in this suggests a legacy of thinking informed by the smaller project. What new strategies have you adopted as the scale of your work has grown from domestic projects to something like the MSCS Building?

PC: We found that there was a transition from doing what we knew about building studwork – the whole NZS 3604 thing. When we moved into larger buildings we had to re-learn a few things. One was the issue of structure and skin. In studwork, you bury any structure you need into it. This affects the way you draw and I think it took us some time to learn another way of drawing. There are some things we learnt the hard way. We designed the Honda Building on Broadway [Newmarket, Auckland] so that the glazing butted into the side of the steel fabricated columns. This was fine until you think about the assembly sequence and discover that the steel work isn't exactly straight. It's not always exactly where you thought it was going to be when you go to fit the glass with tolerances of the width of a silicon joint. That can be up to 25mm but it's not particularly good looking at 25mm. If you take that same detail and shift the glass line out or back to separate these things, you can build in some tolerance. You have freed up the steelwork to move a little and the whole weathering issue is the glazing man's problem. He doesn't have to argue with the steel fabricator over whether the angle is in the right place. That's not to say that we don't put windows in walls because, of course, we do but we learnt to think carefully about how these things happen.

Tectonically the timber stud wall can be a fairly mute element. As you said, the load-bearing structure is typically buried and gib linings rendered seamlessly with no hint of infill or panel suggested. If more tectonic articulation is possible through the separation of the trades, is an understanding of componentry important?

PC: Obviously, but there is also another lesson to learn: recognising where the crossover is between one methodology and another. You have to be careful not to take this strategy of separation all the way to its logical conclusion, which is the dumb commercial building. You make a frame and put a skin around it and that's that.

There are possibilities for richness in the crossover. The MSCS Building's riverside elevation, where you have both structural elements and the glass skin playing key roles in the elaboration of the façade, would appear to be an example of this crossover.

"When we moved into larger buildings we actually had to re-learn a few things. One of those things was the issue of structure and skin."

Mathematics Statistics and Computer Sciences Building

PC: We wanted to make that elevation like a screen. We had the two shear walls at each end making a frame and the floor units extending past them to cover a colonnade. The floor beams are set out flush with the glazing and extend past the ends of the elevation, and the columns are set back so that the glass runs past them. We then took the normal vertical fins from the mullions inside and designed them to go on the outside, shaped like cruciforms and tapered vertically and horizontally. They overlap the floor beams, top and bottom, and also extend beyond the ends, which is part of the language of Canterbury. There are various buildings that have these crossed joints at the ends.

The tectonic interplay in the riverside elevation contrasts the shear walls of the academic office towers. They show a predilection for a kind of eloquent monolithic construction. You are drawn to the idea that you make a wall that holds the building up, lines and clads all at once, difficult though this is. The simple concrete tilt slab is the closest local version of this. You used a higher performance version in the insulated Thermomass panels that make up the academic offices. How hard were they to achieve?

Malcolm Bowes: It was actually difficult, especially in a climate where there's not a lot of this stuff being done – Auckland, for example. It's fair to say that while they look like an incredibly clear and simple way of achieving something, they proved to be difficult to achieve for a number of reasons. The basic idea about Thermomass is very straightforward. You have concrete on the inside, insulation in the middle and concrete on the outside. The challenge starts when you want to have a solid end to close out the panel, as you can see on the academic office towers of the MSCS Building. The end is cast integrally and the return window unit is used to seal the insulation junction. The basic principle is simple and comes from cool store technology but when it comes to all the details, the closed ends and the pointy ends, which need to be reinforced, it gets tricky.

In the New Lynn Community Centre, the insulated wall panels, which I believe were made on site, have window openings with rather subtle and irregularly formed reveals.

PC: Yes, as you walk along them they fold in and form shadows. It's a chance to show you something about the depth. The shear walls at Canterbury were originally 500mm deep so we thought we had to take advantage of this opportunity, to articulate the slot windows in some way. It's not every day that you get to do that. They are just beautiful walls.

You have used this pre-cast concrete technology a number of times now and each time refinements and developments occur. How do you see this work evolving?

Mathematics Statistics and
Computer Sciences Building

PC: In Europe they are doing some superb pre-cast work with different coloured aggregates and cements. We discovered, in the end, that what makes it viable is using locally sourced materials. For example, the gravel and sand in the MSCS Building comes from the Canterbury Plains. In New Lynn we used coloured concrete as the matrix for the panels, made on site. That was tricky because you can't make an aggregate panel tilt up. They were made in beds, and you take them out to release the fines out of the aggregate.

It seems apparent that the aesthetic of technology doesn't interest you for its own sake. In your talk at UNITEC, you mentioned a sort of humanistic technology and we see this in quite a number of projects with passive systems, natural ventilation and earth berms for noise control, that sort of thing. It strikes me that there is a commitment to sustainable technology in a liberating or emancipatory sense rather than a stylistic interest. Can you elaborate?

PC: I think it creates ways in which the architect becomes more involved in the process as opposed to the outcome. The design becomes more holistic; connecting and organising a whole lot more meaning, services and structure. You can open up a lot more of the building to architecture and there is ample opportunity to be more involved. We go along to a meeting and a client says, "Why is this like this?" We can say "Well, the form is really effective and it's dealing with light, it's moving the air, it's highly insulated." I think it has given our relationships with clients a much better footing from which to describe ourselves as 'master builders'.

MT: I think it's fundamental to be interested in creating well-tempered environments. It's what architecture is about. When we started getting into big buildings we naturally assumed that we were interested in these issues.

PC: We try to embrace the technical, and not worry too much about necessarily pursuing the latest technology. We've really been unafraid of the technical. We certainly aren't afraid of services engineers.

Jeanette Budgett is a senior lecturer at the School of Architecture, UNITEC, teaching in design studio and construction technology. Research interests include contemporary and digital fabrication techniques. Practised in residential and school design in Auckland and was a design tutor at the School of Architecture, University of Auckland since graduating in 1986.

"I think it's fundamental to be interested in creating well-tempered environments. It's what architecture is about."

Architectus
Chronology

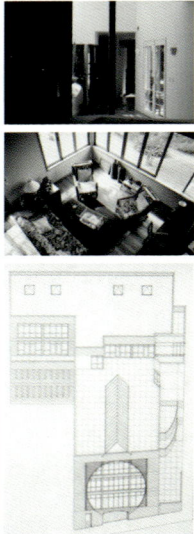

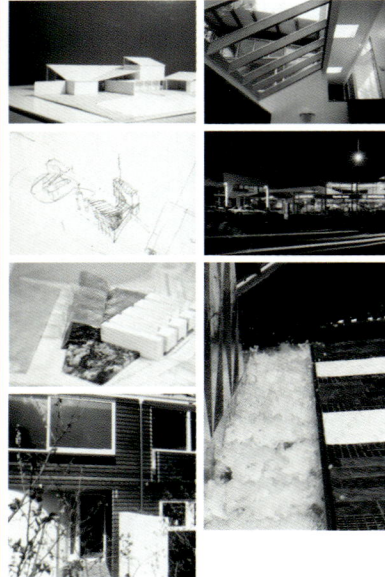

1992

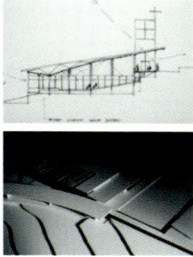

Methodist Church
Waiake, North Shore
*Competition
Submission*

UNITEC Recreation
Centre, Auckland
*Competition
Submission*

1993

House at Medlands
Beach, Great Barrier
Island

House at Te Horo,
Wellington

FHE Gallery
(in association
with Dorita Hannah)
Auckland

1994

Public toilets in Mt Eden,
for Auckland City:
– Stokes Road
– Bellwood Avenue
– Potters Park

University of Canterbury,
Sciences West Precinct
Competition,
Christchurch

1995

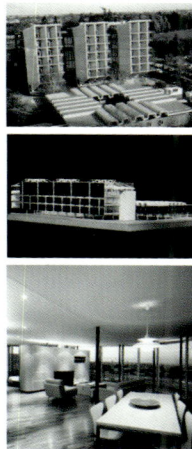

University of
Canterbury, MSCS
Building, Christchurch

University of
Canterbury, Sciences
Library, Christchurch
Project

Apartment at Remuera
Road, Auckland

1996

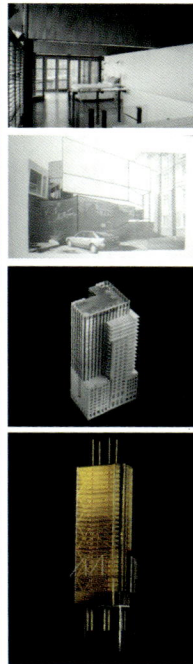

Additions to the Blue
Bach, Bay of Islands

Victoria University Art
Gallery, Wellington
*Competition
Submission*

High-rise Proposals,
Wellington (in
association with
Architecture Workshop
and Billy Apple)
Studies

1997

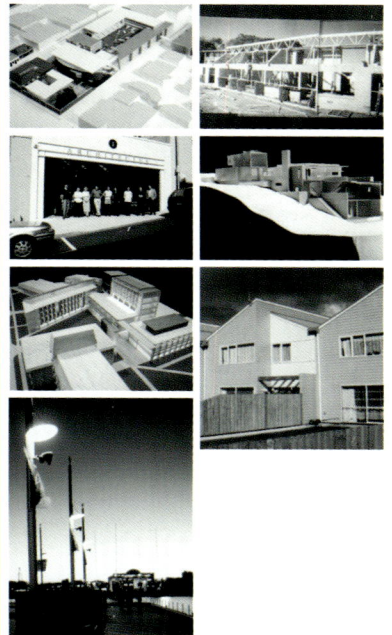

Manawatu Polytech
Development,
Palmerston North
*Competition
Submission*

Architectus Offices,
Centre Street
Auckland

University of
Canterbury,
Psychology Building,
Christchurch
*Competition
Submission*

Waitemata Waterfront,
Public Open Spaces,
Auckland

House at Waiheke
Island, Auckland

House at Stanley Point,
Auckland

Rowena Crescent
Housing, Development
for Housing New
Zealand, Auckland

Architectus
Chronology

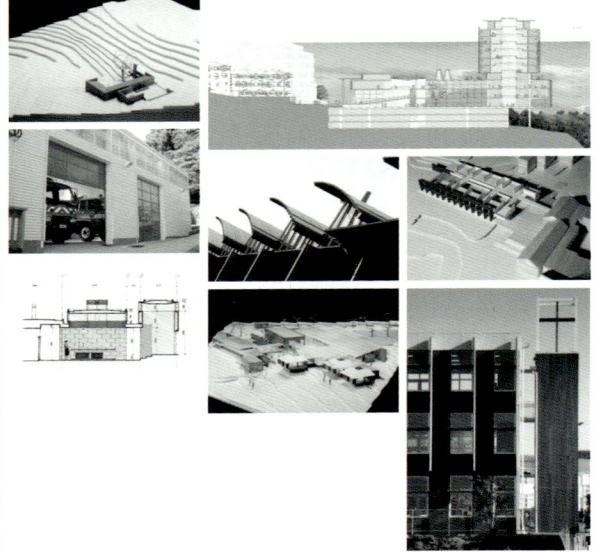

2002

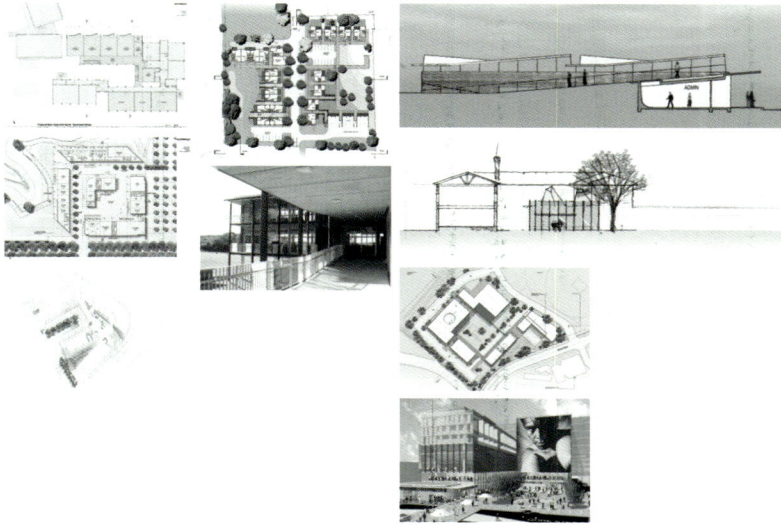

Auckland Grammar School, New Specialist Science Block & Science Block Alterations, Auckland

Town Square for Highbrook Industrial Park, East Tamaki

The University of Auckland Tamaki Campus, Population Health Complex, Auckland

Housing New Zealand New Windsor Road Development, Auckland

Sacred Heart College, New Technology Block & Middle School, Auckland

Nga Whare Waatea Urban Marae, Dining and Function Facility, South Auckland

UNITEC School of Architecture, Alterations, Auckland

The University of Auckland Tamaki Campus, Research Partners Precinct, Auckland

Britomart Above Ground Development (with Trans Tasman Properties) *Development Submission*

2003

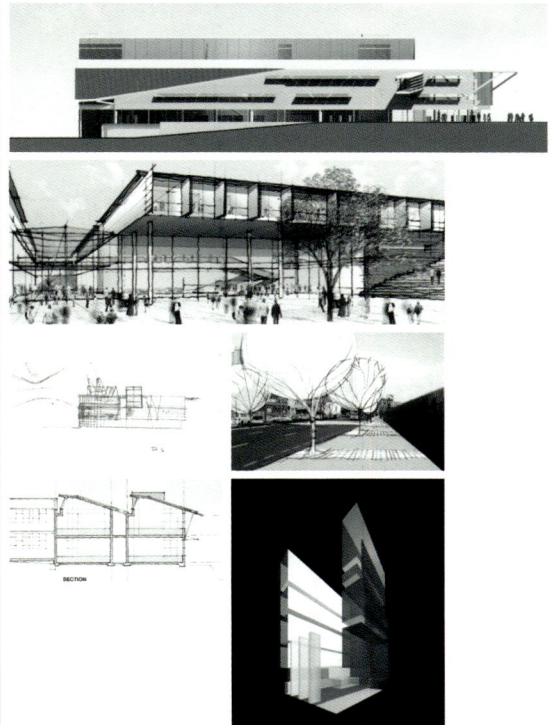

New Henderson Library & UNITEC Building, Waitakere City

The University of Auckland Tamaki Campus, Campus Expansion Building, Auckland

Waitakere City Council Civic Centre, Waitakere City

Northcote College New Sciences Laboratories, North Shore

CBD Streetscape Revitalisation, Auckland

High-Rise Building, Beijing, China

Consultants/Credits

TE PAPA TONGAREWA MUSEUM OF NEW ZEALAND

Client: Competition Entry

Collaborators:
Cook Hitchcock & Sargisson,
Ross Jenner, John Scott, Works
Consultancy

Photographer: Bill Nicol (model)

CLIFFORD/FORSYTH HOUSE

Client:
Patrick Clifford and Leslie Forsyth

Contractor:
Trendsetter Builders Limited,
John Jordan

Structural Engineer:
Brown & Thomson

Photographers:
Patrick Reynolds, Paul McCredie

SCIENCES LIBRARY

Client:
University Of Canterbury

Collaborators:
Cook Hitchcock & Sargisson,
Royal Associates

Structural Engineer:
Holmes Consulting Limited

Services Engineer:
Ove Arup & Partners New Zealand
Limited

Acoustic Consultant:
Marshall Day Acoustics

Quantity Surveyor:
Shipston Davies Limited

Photographer:
Becky Nunes (model)

MATHEMATICS STATISTICS & COMPUTER SCIENCES BUILDING

Client:
University Of Canterbury

Collaborators:
Cook Hitchcock & Sargisson, Royal
Associates

Contractor:
Naylor Love (Canterbury) Limited

Structural Engineer:
Holmes Consulting Limited

Services Engineer:
Ove Arup & Partners New Zealand
Limited

Acoustic Consultant:
Marshall Day Acoustics

Quantity Surveyor:
Shipston Davies Limited

Photographers:
Studio LaGonda,
Duncan Shaw Brown

JADE STADIUM

Client:
Jade Stadium Ltd

Collaborators:
Athfield Architects, Ellerbe Becket

Contractors:
Fletcher Construction Limited /
Chas S Luney Limited

Structural Engineers:
Connell Wagner Limited / Alan Reay
Consultants Limited

Mechanical Engineers:
Beca Carter Hollings & Ferner
Limited

Electrical Engineer:
Pederson Read Limited

Fire Engineer:
Holmes Fire & Safety

Surveyor:
Davie, Lovell-Smith Limited

Project Managers:
Beca Carter Hollings & Ferner
Limited

Quantity Surveyor:
Rawlinsons Limited

Photographer:
Stephen Goodenough

111 WELLESLEY ST.

Client:
Sales Technologies Limited

Contractor:
Haydn & Rollett Construction
Limited

Structural Engineer:
Harris Consulting Limited

Services Engineer:
Ove Arup & Partners New Zealand
Limited

Quantity Surveyor:
Brown & Quartermaine

Photographers:
Patrick Reynolds, Simon Devitt

NETBALL COURT COVER

Client:
Auckland College of Education

Contractor:
Teak Construction Limited

Structural Engineer:
Holmes Consulting Limited

Services Engineer:
Ove Arup & Partners New Zealand
Limited

Quantity Surveyor:
Page Kirkland NZ Limited

Photographer: Simon Devitt

TEACHER SUPPORT SERVICES CENTRE

Client:
Auckland College of Education

Contractor:
Teak Construction Limited

Structural Engineer:
Holmes Consulting Limited

Services Engineer:
Ove Arup & Partners New Zealand
Limited

Quantity Surveyor:
Page Kirkland NZ Limited

Photographer: Michael Ng

**ST PETER'S COLLEGE
NEW TECHNOLOGY BUILDING**

Client:
Roman Catholic Bishop of Auckland

Contractor:
Bracewell Construction Limited

Structural Engineer:
Structure Design Limited

Services Engineer:
Ove Arup & Partners New Zealand
Limited

Fire Engineer:
MacDonald Barnett Partners Limited

Acoustic Consultant:
Marshall Day Acoustics

Quantity Surveyor:
Frank Pinson & Associates Limited

Photographer: Simon Devitt

**ST PETER'S COLLEGE
MIDDLE SCHOOL**

Client:
Roman Catholic Bishop of Auckland

Contractor:
Argon Construction Limited

Structural Engineer:
Structure Design Limited

Services Engineer:
Connell Mott MacDonald Limited

Fire Engineer:
MacDonald Barnett Partners Limited

Acoustic Consultant:
Marshall Day Acoustics

Surveyor:
Connell Wagner Limited

Arborist: Greenscene

Project Manager:
Wallace Associates Limited

Quantity Surveyor:
Dean Murray and Partners

Photographer: Simon Devitt

NEW LYNN COMMUNITY CENTRE

Client:
Waitakere City Council

Contractor:
Watts and Hughes Construction
Limited

Structural Engineer:
Structure Design Limited

Services Engineer:
Ove Arup & Partners New Zealand
Limited

Landscape Architect:
Boffa Miskell Limited

Project Manager:
Waitakere City Council

Quantity Surveyor:
Rawlinsons Limited

Photographer:Simon Devitt

STANLEY POINT HOUSE

Contractor:
Good Brothers Construction Limited

Structural Engineer:
Thorne Dwyer Structures Limited

Landscape Architect:
Rod Barnett

Quantity Surveyor:
Page Kirkland NZ Limited

Photographer:
Patrick Reynolds

**ENGINEERING & SCIENCE
RESEARCH CENTRE**

Client:
The University of Auckland

Contractor:
Aspec Construction Limited

Structural Engineer:
Structure Design Limited

Services Engineer:
Sinclair Knight Merz Limited

Planning Consultant:
Haines Planning Consultants Limited

Security Consultant:
Batchelor Associates Limited

Project Manager:
University of Auckland Property
Services

Quantity Surveyor:
Project Economics Limited

Photographer: Simon Devitt

POPULATION HEALTH COMPLEX

Client:
The University of Auckland

Cultural Consultant:
Rewi Thompson

Contractor:
Fletcher Construction Limited

Structural Engineer:
Structure Design Limited

Services Engineer:
Connell Mott MacDonald Limited

Acoustic Consultant:
Hegley Acoustic Consultants Limited

Planning Consultant:
Haines Planning Consultants Limited

Security Consultant:
Batchelor Associates Limited

Telecommunications Consultant:
Willis Consulting Limited

Landscape Architect:
Halligan Associates

Project Manager:
Carson Group Limited

Quantity Surveyor:
Project Economics Limited

Photographers: Simon Devitt,
Becky Nunes (model)

Architectus
1986-2003

Malcolm Bowes
Patrick Clifford
Michael Thomson

John Sinclair

Carsten Auer
Richard McGowan
James Mooney
Juliet Pope
Jane Priest

Sarah Abbott
Lance Adolph
Justine Ansley
Kellee Aspinall
Aaron Barrett
Sinead Behan
Steven Bird
Iain Blanshard
Andrew Bull
Mark Campbell
Jackie Canning
Keith Carver
Kamal Chaudary
Fiona Christian
Frank Coleman
Barry Condon
Annabel Corbett

Ken Crossan
Mahendra Daji
Stephen de Vrij
Louise Doughty
Sharon Down
Mandy Drummond
James Eades
Nick Easterbrook
Megan Edwards
Adrienne Ewen
Kris Farrier
Prue Fea
James Fenton
Darren Flower
Alex Freyer
Helene Furijan
Sam Gavin
Michael Gould
Peter Greenall
Phillip Guy
Kylie Harris
Joanna Hay
Sophie Hermann
Sharon Ilton
Jonathan Kennedy
Sean Kirton
John Lambert
Lin Lin
Michael Lin

Julie Lincoln
Marc Lithgow
Melanie Lochore
Tai Maki
Emer Maughan
Edward Mayes
Mike McColl
Blair McKenzie
Tania McLachlan
Alan McLeod
Sean McMahon
Tim Mein
Ann Milbank
Bruce Milson
Misako Mitchell
Colette Mullins
Jenny Murdoch
Kennya Nagasse
Gunborg Neovius-Howe
Kirsty Nicol
Ognena Nikolovska
James Noble
Timothy Noton
Robin O'Donnell
Kathryn Pettit
Pru Pinfold
Tadek Rajwer
Tina Rebholz
Giles Reid

Alexis Rochas
Michelle Roe
Jane Rooney
Rachael Rush
Rod Sellers
Elizabeth Seuseu
Michael Shore
Jennifer Sinclair-Ross
Fiona Small
Stephen Smith
Raymond Soh
Linda Steele
Andrea Stevens
Paul Stewart
John Strickland
Nicki Sumicz
Ngata Tapsell
Diane Taylor
Jeremy Thompson
Chrystal Thornton
Lucy Tietjens
Anne Tyng
Gerry Tyrell
Bernard Wind
Emily Winstone
Simon Woodall
Ken Yeung
Mark Yong
Paula Yu

Over 17 years Architectus have collaborated with, or had a close association with many people. We have endeavoured to list them all below and apologise for any omissions. It does not include the many others who have contributed in some ways to Architectus' efforts and we take this opportunity to thank them.

Jane Aimer
Jim Akehurst
Billy Apple
Architecture Workshop
Arup Associates
Athfield Architects
Ian Athfield
Rod Barnett
Peter Boardman
Mathew Bradbury
Diane Brand
Geoff Brimblecombe

Brown & Thomson
Franc Coles
Connell Mott MacDonald
Cook Hitchcock
& Sargisson
Marshall Cook
Ian Dickson
Ellerbe Becket
Dave Fullbrook
Stu Gibson
Richard Goldie
Keith Green

Dorita Hannah
Terry Hitchcock
Graeme Hoddinott
Holmes Consulting
Gary James
Ross Jenner
Stacey Jones
Christopher Kelly
Alistair Knowles
David Murphy
Lindley Naismith
Karen Pettigrew

Royal Associates
Bill Royal
Perry Royal
Mike Sabatini
Peter Sargisson
John Scott
Structure Design
Rewi Thompson
Thorne Dwyer
Steve Thorne
Graeme Voysey
Works Consultancy